"...please just know that your article really made me worry just a little bit less and for today at least, has motivated me further to get the things done that I need to get done so I can get over there too! Grazie!" Dorina

"I was very struck by your article. It seemed to sum [up] many of the feelings I have right now about living in a different country and how invigorating it is." Lauren S.

"I read your article, and i think what u and your husband did is wonderful." Pablo H.

"Can someone with very limited and I do mean limited Italian survive fairly well, although I'm a good traveler [I'm] not sure that I'm ready for the madness that is the Eternal City." John M.

"I read your article on transitionsabroad.com and it was very inspiring and helpful..." Shawn N.

"Your beautiful depiction of living in Rome prompts me to write. I want to work in Rome and I dream of living in Trastevere..." Trycia

"I want to say that you and your husband were so brave to actually make such a huge decision regarding your life and job when moving to another country..." Lindsey M.

"I am planning on moving to Italy in June...I came across your article in transitions abroad and decided you may be able to offer some useful tips." Chere W.

"I just wanted to let you know your story is quite inspiring!!" Amy G.

"I read your column online about moving to Italy, and I was extremely relieved that someone has already done what I am planning on doing." Paul C.

"It was so refreshing to read how you went and followed your dream. It was like I was reading exactly how my boyfriend and I feel." Shani E.

"I just stumbled on your article on living in Rome and I absolutely love it! I am seriously considering moving to Rome next year. And I was curious if you had any special pointers? Thanks very much again for writing a very encouraging and cute article!" Irene C.

"I am writing to you because I want to visit Rome soon and have similar objectives as you and your husband...There's no trust fund here either, just a few dollars in the bank..." Lindy M.

Times New Roman

*How We Quit Our Jobs, Gave Away Our Stuff
& Moved to Italy*

Martha Miller

Published by NJM Press

Library of Congress Cataloging-In-Publication Data
Times new roman: how we quit our jobs, gave away our stuff & moved to Italy
/ Martha Miller— 1st ed.
ISBN: 978-0-9977573-1-6
eISBN: 978-0-9977573-0-9

WC: 46,528
1. Memoir. 2. Travel. 3. Rome. 4. Italy. 5. Happiness.

Formatted in Garamond by Shawn Mihalik
Cover design by Bradford Gantt
Cover photo courtesy of Marty Bushue
Author photo by Doug Carter Images
Printed in the USA

For Nate

*Times New Roman: How we quit our jobs, gave away our stuff &
moved to Italy* is a memoir of the nearly two years my husband
and I lived in Rome, Italy, August 2001 – May 2003. The title,
Times New Roman, has two meanings. First, John and I, in
effect, act as new Romans by transplanting ourselves and
becoming inhabitants of Rome, at least for 21 months. Second,
Times New Roman is a well-known font type, which represents
my realized dream of becoming a published writer while living
in Rome. In some instances, names were changed to protect
the privacy of friends.

TABLE OF CONTENTS

Times New Roman

Dreams come true. Without that possibility, nature would not incite us to have them.

–John Updike

Prologue

I was on vacation with my mother in Florence, Italy, in 1997 when she suggested we hop on a city bus, "...just to see where it takes us." That fortuitous moment changed my life forever.

On the ride up a mountain north of Florence we enjoyed vistas beautiful enough to write home about. We saw postcard-worthy shots all along the route. When we reached Fiesole on the top of the mountain, we set out to explore the city. For us, exploring meant wandering through churches, window-shopping, enjoying a glass of wine *al fresco*, and then deciding on a spot for dinner.

During the shopping portion of our journey, we were surveying the delectable treats in a chocolate shop when we met a thirty-something couple from the United States. My mother was chatting with them when they revealed something amazing: They were not tourists—or "travelers," as Mom and I liked to refer to ourselves—but residents of Fiesole.

My ears perked up and everything, including the warm, intoxicating smell of cocoa, faded into the background. In that moment I thought: *They live here. How did they do it? What do they do for a living? Are they rich? Could I do it, too?* All of these questions and more swirled in my head like the turning vats of dark chocolate in the shop. I stood there too dumbfounded to ask them.

From that moment on, something inside me changed. A seed of possibility was planted. *If they could do it, maybe I can too*, I thought. But it didn't take long for that pessimistic devil to show up and make me doubt this could be my life: *You can't do this. They must have lots of money or special skills. You could never do this.*

I felt unworthy. I didn't want to move to Italy to study art or architecture or ancient civilizations or for any noble cause really. My motivation was so simple it was embarrassing. I had visited one other time and had fallen in love with Italy. I was tempted by the taste of authentic Italian fare, seduced by the sound of its Romance language, awakened by the sight of overflowing flower boxes, cheered by the sight of overhanging laundry lines and, most of all, delighted by the Old-World charm of the people I encountered.

I said to myself: *Forget about the ex-pat couple and the dream. I don't speak the language and don't know anyone in Italy. My career doesn't translate here either. How would I get along? Quit my job? What? Am I crazy?*

I figured that this dream would have to wait until retirement. But then it didn't.

Twenty years from now you will be more disappointed by the things you didn't do than by the ones you did. So throw off the bowlines. Sail away from the safe harbor. Catch the trade winds in your sails. Explore. Dream. Discover.

–Mark Twain

The 21-Month Plan

My husband and I are not trust-fund babies or self-made millionaires, but like many people, we dreamed of living abroad. In August 2001, after much discussion, research, and planning (which included John's ceiling to baseboard flowchart of To-Dos), we boarded a plane departing from Houston, Texas, en route to Rome, Italy. Checking only the allowable two bags each — one of which contained a bicycle — we began what we referred to as the "21-Month Plan."

This unconventional adventure was not funded by a corporate overseas assignment, an inheritance or winning lottery ticket, but in lots of little money-saving ways, such as brown-bagged lunches and bypassed caffé mochas.

When I first met my husband-to-be in 1998, I overheard him musing about quitting his job and living in a box on a beach in Mexico. I was immediately skeptical but secretly intrigued. Fast forward two years and there we were, enjoying our honeymoon in Guadalajara. No, we didn't stay in a box; he actually sprang for a hotel suite. However, before we got married, we did discuss the "box on the beach" idea — endlessly.

The "box" was upgraded to a more stable dwelling and European countries were added to our pool of choices. We had enough money saved to bum around for a while. *But then what?* John was forty-two and I was thirty-seven when we started planning this adventure. We were too old to throw caution to the wind and too young to retire. We wanted to live somewhere and not feel like tourists in city after city. I wanted to know my neighbors and understand what their lives were like. We needed a plan that would not only allow us to experience another culture, but also prepare us for future earnings.

John had spent twenty-five years in television news and was ready to build on his experience and try something new. He decided to further his education and pursue a degree in international affairs. That decision was the catalyst that made us realize we could, actually should, move abroad. It would take twenty-one months for John to graduate and it was a goal that would give us long-term stability, a home base. My background was in retail sales and marketing. Learning another language would open new doors for me as well, though not in the way I had originally thought.

But can we afford to quit our jobs? I wondered. John would be going back to school full time. Neither of us spoke any other languages, which meant I wouldn't be able to work abroad right away, if at all. We had to make sure we had enough money put aside to cover John's tuition, our housing costs, living expenses, plus an allotted amount for emergencies. Our plan could not include traveling back to the United States unless there was an urgent need. The 21-Month Plan was going to require a significant chunk of change and, once we started, we agreed there would be no turning back.

We also agreed that our retirement savings accounts were off limits. We would have to fund this venture in other ways. We didn't have kids and we didn't own a home. We also didn't have any credit-card debt and our cars were fully paid for. John had been effective at living beneath his means for years; he was a disciplined saver. Having my job eliminated not once, but twice, I had learned the value and peace of mind of a healthy cushion of savings.

John and I married in 2000. As we combined our households, our expenses decreased. Rent alone resulted in a savings of $500 per month. We challenged ourselves with a hefty goal to add to our savings. We found that saving for something as specific as living abroad made it a whole lot easier to make sacrifices, big and little. For example, Starbucks caffè mochas were one of my favorite treats. But during the year before we moved to Rome, I reminded myself as I drove past their stores on my way to work, for each caffè mocha I passed on now, I could enjoy three Italian *cappuccini* later.

After our honeymoon, John began researching English-language, degree-granting universities on the Internet. We evaluated the cities based on our interest in the culture, language and cost of living. The final candidates were in Madrid and Rome. We knew we would not be able to make such enormous changes in our lives without at least one visit to ease our minds about this adventure. We planned a vacation in

March 2001 to visit both cities for the final winnowing. One of the universities in Rome fulfilled all of our requirements. We were even shown some apartments during our visit. By choosing one that normally houses only one student, we could trim costs. We left a housing deposit for the fall semester before we departed. I said, "This is the turning point—we are really going to do this."

For months as we were trying to decide if we should take the risk of quitting our jobs and moving to Italy, several thoughts kept going through my mind: *Two years are going to go by anyway. How are we going to feel in two years if we don't take this chance? What about in twenty years? Will we always have nagging feelings of "What if....?"*

Happily, we will never have to ask ourselves these questions. Our son, however, born after this adventure, may someday ask us what happened to his inheritance.

To be without some of the things you want is an indispensable part of happiness.

–Bertrand Russell

Downsizing, in More Ways Than One

Quitting your job and moving abroad has a devil-may-care sound to it. It's impulsive, romantic and adventurous. Sure, I'd like to think those words describe us and maybe they do to some extent, but the reality is that we are practical people. We have devoted an enormous amount of thought and effort into our 21-Month Plan.

One of the first moves I made was to consult my financial advisor, who is in charge of my IRA, a 401k brought over from a previous downsizing. Ken was a laid-back Southerner who chose his words carefully. I was more nervous when John and I bound into his office to get his reaction to our plan than I was when I told my friends and my parents.

I knew if Ken deemed this plan to be a poor financial decision, and downright foolish, it would have caused me to reconsider, and I didn't want to do that. But I knew he'd be straight with me, so his reaction was crucial. At first, I was so giddy. "Guess why we're here," I tease. "You're having a baby?" he asks.

"Nope."

"You want to buy a house?"

"No," I say. "We want to quit our jobs and move to Europe so John can finish his education and we can experience living abroad."

Ken's eyes widen, his mouth turns into a smile and he uncharacteristically blurts out, "Oh, thank goodness. I thought you were going to say you wanted to buy a boat!"

Having Ken's blessing was essential to me. As long as he thought we would be able to afford it; that was all I needed to hear. It was the equivalent of Suze Orman's, "You're APPROVED, Girlfriend!"

When we got back from the March 2001 trip to Madrid and Rome for the final winnowing, John's television station announced that it would be conducting voluntary buyouts over the next several months. This wasn't completely unexpected news. John had had a feeling this would happen and he immediately put in for it, although it would be May before we found out if he was chosen. The timing could not have been better. If John were chosen, he would have several months during the summer to get us ready for the move and his severance package would boost our savings and provide a few more months of paychecks to cover our living expenses in Italy. Everything seemed to say that we were making the right decision. I worked right up until we left to maximize my earnings, and I banked my vacation days so those would be paid out after I left my job.

While we waited to hear from John's employer, we began working on checking off the "To Dos" on that lengthy list that hung in the spare bedroom. One of the first things I wanted to take care of was the documentation I needed to live in Italy. This required me to visit the *Consolato Generale d'Italia a Houston*, the Italian Consulate, to make sure we had all the documentation we would need for me to stay. (If you're planning to stay longer than 90 days, a special visa is required.) For John it was simple: he could obtain a student visa. I was applying for a spousal visa.

This is going to be easy, I thought. *I have months to get this done.*

On my first visit, I noticed a young woman literally sweating about getting her student visa in time. I overheard her say she was scheduled to depart in a couple of days and the Consulate was giving her no hope of having her visa approved that quickly. Taking this as a clear warning, I thought to myself: *Do not let that be you.* With months to go, I knew I would not wait until the last minute as she had to get something so important taken care of. That was just not me! Or so I thought.

I visited the Consulate several times over the following months. Each time, I had to use my lunch hour to drive from the Medical Center to the Consulate's office on Post Oak, which is near the Galleria. It was less than eight miles one way but Houston traffic can be treacherous. The office's posted hours were not always observed. And even if the door was unlocked, I was not always successful in being seen because others were already there, waiting in line. This meant I had to come back another day. Making an appointment was not an option; they didn't take appointments. When I finally did get to talk to someone, it seemed no matter what documentation I brought, the person I met with asked for something else, such as our marriage license. When I presented the marriage license on the next visit, I was told it needed to be translated into Italian. I had to send off for that, pay a few dollars, and then wait a month to have a new certificate issued and mailed to us because the Consulate's office did not perform that service.

Once I had the Italian marriage license in hand, they asked to see our bank statements that showed how much money we had to live on. They wanted to verify we would not be a drain on the Italian economy. *Mamma mia!* I should have taken all this as a sign of things to come. It was excellent training in Italian bureaucracy.

Besides scurrying to the Italian Consulate once every couple of weeks, we started chipping away at the other "To-Dos" on the list:

- ○ Consolidate bank accounts

- ○ Send tuition and housing payments for the first semester

- ○ Prepare to shut off utilities

- ○ Give notice to vacate apartment

- ○ Change mailing address

- ○ Figure out where to change our mailing address to

- ○ Book plane tickets to Rome

And on and on and on. One of the items on the list read: "Downsize stuff," which was not easily checked off. We had so much stuff. It took months to go through it all and weed out what was not needed, not special, not sentimental.

John and I had accumulated years of stuff, and when we moved in together we combined our stuff and got a larger apartment to house it all. It would have been smarter to downsize before we got married so we could have rented a smaller place and saved more money for this adventure but unfortunately, we didn't do that.

We were determined that we would not spend one cent on a storage facility, not even if it cost as little as $100 a month. That would have been $2,100!!! There was no way we were doing that.

Fortunately, we had incredible friends and family who were willing to store some of our necessities and favorite items. My dad and his wife, Joy, lived in East Texas and they had room for our washer and dryer, my sewing machine and a few boxes of Christmas decorations. We took a mountain bike to Austin, Texas, where Chris, one of John's five brothers, lived so he could use it while we were gone. Close friends Suzy and Rick gave lodging to a leather sofa, our bed, a large archival box that held my wedding dress, and an antique, wooden church pew John had acquired before we met. The pew found a home in their entryway where it continues to reside long after our stay in Italy and return to the U.S. It would never look as good anywhere else nor would it be taken care of as well by anyone else, including us. Other close friends Cynthia and Richard housed random pieces: lamps, a wicker table and two chairs, and a funky end table with curved legs I had bought at a yard sale Cynthia and I stopped at a few years before.

John and I could've had a yard sale ourselves, save for the fact that we didn't have a yard. Besides, I knew we wouldn't make much money from the effort, so I spent many a weekend sorting, loading, and hauling smaller household and personal items to donate to a shop that benefits a battered women's shelter. I dropped some items off at a consignment shop, and found a resale housewares shop that gave me a pittance for several place settings of china that I had had for years, but that had only been used one or twice. Instead of feeling bad about the little cash all this effort produced, I felt freer having the stuff gone.

Michael, a friend from work, brought me a large roll of bubble wrap to pack my stemware, which I felt compelled to keep although the occasion to pull out such fragile glassware rarely, if ever, occurred. In gratitude, I gave him a pink, Depression-era, glass bowl my mother had handed down to me. Michael is a collector of glass *objet d'art* and was absolutely thrilled. I should have felt bad giving away something my mother had given me, but the piece wasn't something I would have chosen, and I never used it. It made me happy for Michael to have it.

A few days later, Michael reported that he had researched the price of the bowl and discovered it was worth around $60. He was beside himself with glee, and I had the pleasure of knowing that someone I like was going to enjoy that Depression-era piece more than I ever would.

In May, we received the excellent news that John got the voluntary buyout. *Full steam ahead!* There was truly no turning back.

We spent the rest of the summer doing everything we could think of to ready ourselves for living overseas. We went to dentist and doctor appointments. John sold three more bicycles, and we enrolled in Leisure Learning, Houston's Adult Continuing Education program, to begin learning Italian. It was not a moment too soon, as we had no knowledge of Italian except for a few phrases we had learned from our short visit.

De-cluttering can be exhausting. Sorting through possessions brings up old memories, some good and some not so good, and it requires serious thought. To Keep or Not To Keep piles were made. If it lands in the To Keep pile, I had to decide where I would put it for the next 21 months. If it is placed in Not-To-Keep, is it worth anything? Will I feel guilty if I get rid of it because my mother/ father/sister/friend gave it to me? John kept reminding me of the adage, we are owned by our possessions. I learn how true that is. All this stuff was weighing us down.

Some household items were no brainers. We ditched tchotchkes, *good riddance*. Gave away mismatched drinking glasses, *salute*. And sacked ubiquitous promotional plastic cups, the kind that seem to multiply in the dark recesses of precious kitchen cabinet space, *buh bye!*

Just before we moved, John called the Salvation Army to pick up some larger pieces of furniture and several boxes we were donating. He mistakenly instructed the men to take a few of the boxes I had meant to keep. I was sad for a little while when I realized what had happened, but truth was there were only a couple of small items worth keeping in those boxes and seeing the floor instead of piles of boxes signaled progress. I could live without those things.

Papers! Good Lord! We had files and folders and boxes of receipts and warranties. I spent an entire Saturday organizing the papers we should keep. I put our most important documents together in a slim binder that we would take with us: social security cards, birth certificates, copies of drivers licenses, and all those documents the Consulate requested: copies of bank statements, our marriage license, and the copy of the marriage license in Italian.

Something serendipitous happened the day of the paper purging process. I went to Office Max and bought a $40 shredder. Paper shredders weren't that common then or I'd have borrowed one. Destroying old pay stubs, credit card bills and various work documents was pretty mundane and the noise from the shredder grated (pun intended) on my nerves, and I could not wait to be done. But then I came across some personal journal pages written in spiral notebooks. Some of these entries were written as a way to deal with stress from decades ago. In a moment of impulsiveness, I decided to rid myself of those memories. Watching the pages being cut into strips felt not only good but also cathartic! *Why have I hung onto these memories for years?* I wondered. Seeing them reduced to nothing but lifeless shreds felt so much better than hanging onto the physical documents and the feelings attached to them. At the end of the day I had a sense of peace I never expected. My only regret was not having done it sooner.

I was ready to start journaling about this new, positive phase of my life. I bought an aubergine Flavia journal featuring an hourglass with milky stars acting as sand inside and a few others scattered on the cover. Next to the hourglass was this quote, "Believe in your heart that something wonderful is about to happen." I truly did.

* * *

August was quickly approaching and I still didn't have a visa. I was starting to panic. One late July afternoon I visited the Italian Consulate's office again. The official, a slight, older Italian man with a gentle voice that I had already met with several times seemed weary to see me again. I showed him all my documents again, including bank statements and marriage license translated into Italian. He shook his head, managed a slight smile and sympathetically said, *"Mi dispiace, e non possibile."* I'm sorry, it is not possible. I started to tear up just like the study-abroad girl I swore I wouldn't be like.

Later that afternoon, I called Suzy and told her I didn't know what I would do if I couldn't leave with John in August because it might take a few more weeks to get my visa approved. I asked her if I could stay with her for a little while, if needed. As soon as the words left my mouth, I knew that was not the right thing to do. No matter what, I was leaving with John on August 26 somehow, someway.

The answer finally became clear. It had been right in front of me the whole time. John was eligible for a student visa because he was enrolling in a university. I was going to be studying Italian full time. *Wouldn't that make me a candidate for a student visa as well?* I immediately got on the Internet and searched Italian language schools in Rome. Choosing what I thought looked like the best one, and one I could afford, I made an inquiry through its website and learned I could register online. The school would expedite via FedEx the documentation needed for the Consulate. I plugged in my credit card numbers and charged sixteen weeks of intensive language classes, which would give me a reason to be in Italy for more than ninety days. *Bada bing, bada boom! Done!*

I'll never know for sure if it was presenting the institute's enrollment document or the shameless name-dropping of a prominent Italian businessman I had just met through work, but my student visa was approved two days later. *Grazie a Dio!*

A month before we left, we hired a lawyer to draw up our wills, and we even had our medical directives spelled out, just in case. Three weeks out, I gave notice at my job. The 21-Month Plan had been a covert mission until then.

We hadn't told anyone but our families and a few friends what we were doing. Keeping a secret for nearly a year had weighed on me more than I knew. After spilling the beans and resigning, the rest of the day felt like I'd visited a spa. My shoulders relaxed and the tension I'd been carrying around dissolved, leaving me with a wonderful sense of calmness.

In mid-August, Vincent, another one of John's brothers, flew to Houston from Buffalo, New York, to buy my car, a 1994 Nissan Altima. John sold his red 1990 Toyota pickup. We were excited by the thought of being able to walk and rely on public transportation to get around Rome. Even though I could have easily ridden a city bus to work in Houston, I chose to drive the congested route and pay monthly parking fees for the "convenience" of having my car. I'd rationalized that it was too hot in the summer to wait for the bus. *Besides, what if something came up during the day and I needed to drive somewhere,* I reasoned. I could easily have taken the bus that stopped right in front of my apartment, but never did—not once. What a waste!

We rented a car for the last few days before our departure. Suzy and Rick generously invited us to stay at their house for a couple of nights so we could clean our apartment and relinquish the keys. To me, keys have always signified a beginning or an ending of sorts.

Suzy and Rick hosted a *buon viaggio* party for us at their home on Saturday, August 25, 2001, to give us a chance to say good bye to our friends, and then they drove us to the airport the next day. John and I were so excited and happy. The day had finally come, but I didn't feel the magnitude that we were leaving our friends and families for nearly two years. It felt exactly like we were going on vacation. Besides, I knew that Suzy and Rick and Cynthia and Richard would come to visit, as would members of our families, so it didn't feel like we wouldn't see them again soon.

I had an epiphany of sorts on the flight to Rome. As I looked out the window thousands of feet above the Atlantic, I realized that if the plane went down right now our affairs were in the best order they could possibly be. We had dispersed our belongings, except the two bags we each were bringing, which would surely be lost at sea along with us. We had no residence. No cars. No children. We had wills that designated beneficiaries of our savings and retirement accounts. No one would have to sort through our stuff, choose what we would wear for our funerals, or take care of any of those normal things one takes care of when someone dies. There would be no need for anyone to do anything. We had all of our i's dotted and t's crossed, with not a loose end anywhere. It was an odd feeling, if not morbid—and weirdly satisfying at the same time.

Traveling is the ruin of all happiness! There's no looking at a building after seeing Italy.

—Fanny Burney

Rear Window, Italian Style

27 August 2001

The taxi van delivering us from Fiumicino airport to our new neighborhood in Trastevere cannot fit down the narrow, cobbled street to the building where we are moving. The driver stops at the cross street and motions so there is no misunderstanding that this is as far as he can make it. He helps us unload our bags, one of which is a ginormous bike carrier, and, as soon as we pay him, he speeds off, leaving us to manage our belongings and navigate the rest of the way by ourselves. In the afternoon sun, jet lagged and running on adrenaline, we haul three suitcases and the bike case up the bumpy path to the doorway of Vicolo del Bologna 15. It's surreal that we are moving into our new home at this moment, even after all our planning. It's more of an excited, we're-on-vacation vibe than the major transition we have embarked upon. We don't dare complain; we are too happy to be doing this at all.

John had called Christine, our contact at the university, before we left the airport to let her know that we were on our way so she is waiting for us at the front door with the keys to our new home.

When we had visited Rome the previous spring, the university's housing department showed us four apartments. We had no problem agreeing on this one. Our choice doesn't look out upon the domed city (not that that was an option), but onto a courtyard that affords us a bird's eye view of our neighbors' terraces. We even passed up a larger, two-bedroom place with a view of the Palatine Hill. We intentionally picked a one-bedroom studio (meant to house only one person) because it is perfect for observing the Mediterranean lifestyle we are eager to adopt.

Our five-story walk-up, a building of rich ochre tagged with graffiti on either side of its heavy, dark wooden doors, looks older than any building I've ever lived in. And this may very well be true, if the marker above its doors—the year "1878" rings true. An intercom security system located to the left of the door with a weathered list of tenants scrawled in various colors of ink catches my eye. I take a moment to imagine adding our names to the list and becoming friends with the owners of these Italian names as we cross the threshold and follow Christine into the dim foyer.

Once inside, we drop our bags and carry what we can easily manage up the steep, winding, narrow staircase. When we reach the fourth floor, Christine shows us how to open our door with the key, which is very sturdy and four and a half inches long. When her cellphone rings, she has to leave and makes a quick exit. We are left standing in what will be home for the next twenty-one months. *Have we really done this? Is this where we live now?* The weight of the key in my hand gives me my answer.

The bike case we've transported to this Old World continent is not only an awkward shape—a huge rectangle—but also extra heavy due to the bike and bike tools John has stowed in it for the trip. We are dripping in sweat as we strong-arm the bike case and the rest of our baggage up the marble stairs to the fourth floor and take our first good look around our new home.

The apartment consists of three small rooms, each with tall, French windows that make the rooms feel larger. Dark wooden crossbeams throughout the apartment add support and interest to the stark white stucco walls and ceiling. The layout is peculiar, to say the least; narrow double doors lead from the living room to the bedroom and then shotgun style from the bedroom straight into the kitchen. A step into the kitchen and to the left is the doorway to the bathroom.

The living room furniture includes a small, three-tiered bookshelf, a rectangular, dark wood dining table and four small chairs. A 1960s era armoire with harvest gold plastic paneled doors occupy a good bit of the approximately 8' by 10' room. Four wooden boxes line a wall to form a banquette. The boxes provide needed storage, but the painfully thin cushions make for very uncomfortable seating. I decide to replace the faded, calico-print coverings as soon as possible. A rocking chair takes up the last bit of floor space. The glossy brick-red tile is the prettiest feature of the room—besides the incredible view.

Every balcony of the cantaloupe-colored building we face holds flower boxes and pottery with overflowing foliage. Ivy creeps up to the shingled, terracotta roof and around one side. Latticework dividers attempt to give privacy to two residences that share one of the larger patio spaces. Robust bougainvillea in window boxes line the outer ledges. Outside steps give way to a larger patio and two small upper balconies embellished with ferns in hanging pots. I could stand here all day gazing out this window and never get bored - every inch made beautiful in a natural, not-trying-too-hard way.

Inside, the bedroom is simple. Bookshelves are conveniently recessed into the stucco walls; several English-Italian dictionaries curiously left behind lean against one another. The bed is just a very firm mattress (think hay bale) on a wooden base with no head or footboard. The artwork seems disparate, probably having been left by various tenants over the years. One framed piece holds yellowed paper, perhaps torn from a book, with a dozen or so past popes donning vestments of their era. There are no closets in the apartment, but there is a tall, blond-wood wardrobe. Even with the minimal clothing we've brought, we will easily fill it. In contrast, our bedroom closet in Houston had been large enough for John to store three bicycles!

The bathroom, very small by American standards, is adequate with shower, sink, toilet and bidet. *Bidet? Yes, a sure sign we're not in Texas anymore,* I think.

The bathroom's sole window is charming with its frosted

pane. Anxious to see the view from this angle, I slide open the latch and pull in the window, catching the inhabitants of the window's exterior ledge off guard. Scuffling and warbling rise in protest as roosting pigeons fly away. All the commotion stirs up a face full of feathers, not to mention a smell reminiscent of the hen house at the Houston Live Stock Show and Rodeo. The window ledge is deep, a hollow cavern reaching into the thick walls of the building. It provides a comfortable, cool place to rest for the birds as well as a perch for doing what comes naturally. If we leave the window open, the birds will strut right into the bathroom, I'm sure. With this many birds congregating just outside the bathroom, the window cannot be opened and proves useless at the moment save for the dim light that filters through the frosted pane. *I see a DIY project in our near future*, I think.

The kitchen, better described as a kitchenette, has a miniscule cooking area that contains exactly two modern conveniences: a stove with an oven and refrigerator. No dishwasher, garbage disposal or microwave. Unlike the rich Tuscan tile-covered kitchens I imagine Italians preside over as they demonstrate their pasta-making skills, ours is all white, with a few splashes of color, thanks to the bright orange light fixture that drops from the ceiling and the cherry-colored dish drainer and trashcan. The built-in pantry, a three-shelved alcove between the sink and the stove, adds to the charm and makes it easy to determine when I will have to do grocery shopping or, as I will soon learn to call it, *fare la spesa*.

The pops of color are energizing, but the part I like best is that everything, including the appliances, is proportioned as if made especially for me. My driver's license lists my height as 5'1", but in truth, this is a slight exaggeration. In this kitchen, for the first time in my life, I can easily see the top of a refrigerator and reach everything in the kitchen cabinets— even on the top shelf!

If the rest of Rome is anything like our kitchen, I will fit in perfectly, I muse.

Our first night in Rome

A tiny spider (ack!) hops across the unmade bed. There are no bed linens or towels. I thought they came with, but I'm secretly glad there aren't any so I have an excuse to buy new ones. I tie my leopard print robe around my pillow as a pillowcase and instantly feel better. A co-worker in Houston gave me two washcloths with American flags on them. They are the kind that are packed tightly into little disks the size of quarters and expand in water. They became very precious tonight when I needed to wash the last twenty-four hours off my face.

We are tired this evening, but go shopping for linens anyway. We run out of time as stores begin closing for the day by pulling garage-like doors down and locking up around 8:30. Surprisingly this small act transforms colorful shops into blank walls - a completely different look at night than when they are open for business. We buy cleaning supplies at a little shop around the corner before it pulls its doors closed, drop in on an Internet café to send a brief message to friends and family telling them we've made it, then have dinner across the street from our new home: antipasto and fettuccine with mushrooms, white wine in a little carafe and three mixed scoops of gelato for dessert.

We unpack, compose a shopping list for tomorrow, hook

up the air conditioner (thank goodness), take showers and are finally relaxing; I write in my journal while John reads.

Later that night, as we turn out the bedroom light, glowing white stars, the type used in a baby's nursery, radiate down on us from between the cross beams. In any other setting I would have deemed them out of place and made plans to remove them, but tonight they're just another quirky part of our new home, and they make me smile.

I couldn't settle in Italy—it was like living in a foreign country.
                              −Ian Rush, Welsh soccer player

Fare la Spesa

29 August 2001

Tonight I will make dinner for the first time in our new home. We need this ritual to signal to our brains that we aren't on vacation but that we actually live here now. In Houston, John or I cooked almost every night. We arrived in Rome two days ago and have been so busy getting acclimated that we haven't had time to stock up on the basics. It's been fun trying new foods like pizza with only roasted potato and rosemary for toppings. And then there's gelato. We've eaten more than I want to admit, but again the flavors are new to us: *cassata* − vanilla with candied fruit, and *zabaglione* − egg custard. The creamy texture slides down quickly but doesn't make you feel stuffed.

There are little food markets that carry different assortments tucked in at what seem odd places. At the end of Vicolo del

Bologna one sells limited produce: lemons, tomatoes, arugula, and hazelnuts while another shop that faces Piazza Sant'Egidio carries a fuller line with all of these less the hazelnuts but adding gorgeous purple eggplants, cantaloupes and plastic jugs of apple juice. But this morning we'll make the trek to the local grocery store to fill our kitchen with all the basics. We'll also pick up some breakfast and lunch items and ingredients for tonight's dinner.

John and I head down the three flights of stairs from our new abode. The first step outside is onto paved cobbles. There is no sidewalk as this is a very narrow street, a *vicolo*. This morning, the air is still slightly cool, as most of the city streets and alleys remain shaded by buildings. Through the windows and glass doors of the restaurant that sits across the alley, we can see some of the employees milling about. Two men, one being the owner, we find out later, are leaning against the doorframe and smoking. The smell of tobacco meets us as they smile and nod to us. We smile and nod back.

We amble south on the *vicolo* where we are beckoned by the aroma of freshly ground coffee beans wafting in the open air. Not even trying to resist, we stop in for coffee. As we wait our turn to order, mentally practicing what we need to say in Italian, the glass case with plain and chocolate croissants, fruit turnovers and glazed brioches captures our attention. Agreeing it's not a good idea to grocery shop on an empty stomach, we surrender -- an apple turnover for John and a chocolate croissant (*cornetto*) for me, and *due cappuccini*.

Space at the bar is scarce, but on the opposite wall I secure a seat on a barstool and John stands next to me to eat his breakfast. Several people glide through the open doors, greeting the barista with a rich, throaty *"Buon giorno,"* before downing an espresso or cappuccino and scuttling out the door. I take note of how the women are put together, admiring their trendy outfits accessorized with just-right handbags and jewelry, and their hair is always freshly washed and styled. Known as the *"bella figura,"* it's important to Italians to always look good from head to toe. I'm becoming self-conscious of my comfort-over- style image: sleeveless tee, blue jeans and flat sandals.It's just a short walk to the grocery store, but there is much to take in on this most mundane of errands. We traverse Piazza Santa Maria in Trastevere, a popular gathering place and home to the oldest church in Rome. The gleaming mosaics by Pietro Cavallini shine more brilliantly in the morning sun, and we can't traipse by without paying them proper respect.

A restaurant with outdoor seating does a booming tourist business with tall glasses of freshly squeezed orange juice as the draw. Enormous terracotta planters, with dozens of blood oranges piled high, give the piazza an energizing shot of color. It takes real discipline not to pull up a chair and order one of those enticing beverages, but we're not on vacation we tell each other—we *live* here.

Trying to stay focused on our mission, we stroll past the octagonal fountain and notice one entire side of the piazza is covered in scaffolding. Whether it is true or not, we are later told by Iris, a shop keeper in Trastevere who becomes a good friend, that taxes are not collected during renovations. I look forward to seeing this building without the scaffolding.

As we exit the piazza, a twenty-something man, heavily tattooed, heavily pierced and dressed head to toe in black, holds out a paper cup, collecting change for himself and a large black dog lying nearby. I smile but shake my head and he nods back, seeming to take no offense. Moving on through the adjacent Piazza San Calisto, we admire buildings in terracotta, maize and wine casting a glow like a daylong sunset. Often described as Bohemian, these homes are bedecked with flower boxes and clinging ivy that intertwine with coffee bars, restaurants, and one-of-a-kind boutiques. From the cobblestone streets to the overhanging laundry lines, every step brings another postcard- perfect setting into focus.

We are now on San Francisco a Ripa, the street where Standa, the local outlet of a grocery store chain is positioned. Real estate is at a premium in Rome, and this store is in the basement of an Oviesse store, a chain that reminds me of a small-scale Target with trendy, inexpensive clothing and accessories for men, women and children.

To get to Standa, we must trek through Oviesse, and take the stairs in the middle of the store down through a bookstore also located underground. Exiting the book store – still underground – puts us finally in the grocery store. Once inside, John pulls at the handles of a couple of shopping carts lined up in front of the cashiers, but they are stuck together, and it seems no amount of yanking will free one. A customer approaches with her own shopping cart and uses a "key," a slab of metal about three inches long dangling from the first linked cart, to dislodge a £500 coin in the cart she is returning. Her cart has now joined the conga line, and she slips the coin into her pocket. We realize the carts aren't stuck, but chained together on purpose. First lesson in Italian grocery shopping: Grocery carts are available with a refundable deposit.

We see we've already made a mistake, not merely in trying to untangle the carts, but in failing to carry any coins with us. In the two days since we've arrived, we've already gotten the idea that it is considered a major inconvenience to ask for change. Lira is still the national currency and large bills will get you nothing but rolled eyes and a huff. A Standa cashier notices our fumbling and takes pity, giving us change for our paper bill, £50,000, equivalent to about $25. Lesson two: Bring coins.

Now that we have secured a cart, I breathe a sigh of relief; doing the actual shopping should be easy. The store is laid out similarly to the ones in the U.S. Fruit and vegetables on one side, refrigerated section to the back and candy displays near the three cash registers. We shouldn't have to know another language to do this.

Starting in produce, we gather up tomatoes and lettuce for a salad. Salad dressing, though, is elusive. Looking up and down the aisles, we finally spy a small display rack near the radicchio with exactly two choices. I select a bottle with full fat; there is no low-cal version. No second-guessing, no guilt. Brilliant! I wonder how many years of my life have been spent comparing labels and prices. Regular, no fat, low fat, store brand vs. name brand vs. gourmet brand. Two choices – ahhh. I savor this new simplicity.

When we make it to the dairy section, it becomes necessary to consult our Italian-English dictionary. Unfamiliar labels contain sour cream. Or is that half-and-half? Or unflavored yogurt? Butter, or *burro,* is more obvious, though it doesn't look like the version we buy in the States. It's the size of two large sticks molded together and packaged in waxy paper with no box. Every so often an old friend stands out from the crowd like the tin-foil wrapper of Philadelphia Brand Cream Cheese.

Choosing a basic necessity like milk gets complicated. White one- liter boxes with variously colored labels are neatly stacked on an end cap with no refrigeration. Deciphering the code with our dictionary, we determine the box with sky blue wording is skim milk, or *scremato,* so we add what we soon begin referring to as "box o' milk" to our cart.

Hunting for eggs, literally, nets the hard-to-find orbs at the end of the bottled water aisle, which just seems wrong. And like the milk, they are not refrigerated. There are no egg substitutes either so we indulge in the real thing. It seems like we've been in this store forever, and we haven't checked off many items from our shopping list.

At the seafood counter, huge whole fish lay in wait. I point to the salmon and say, *"Per due persone."* The man in a white apron looks us over and makes the determination of how much that would be and packages it, handing it to me with a broad smile. That was amazingly uncomplicated.

A stop in the deli section is a feast for the eyes. Fresh pesto made with basil and pine nuts is a treat. Thank goodness, I can again just point at the luscious green condiment and the medium-sized plastic containers to let the young woman working the counter know what and how much I want. She flashes a beautiful smile and seems genuinely happy that we are purchasing something of such good quality.

The simplicity of choosing a salad dressing is a distant memory when it's time to select pasta. The entire length of one side of the aisle is devoted to this staple of Italian cuisine. Besides the familiar spaghetti, linguine, fettuccine and penne, scores of exotically shaped varieties— *gemelli, casarecce, orecchio* and shells of every dimension—line the shelves. We vow to try every one during our twenty-one month adventure, but for now we toss *orecchiette* (little ears) and a familiar favorite, spaghetti, into our basket.

The olive oil aisle is equally overwhelming with hundreds of bottles and dozens of brands and grades. All I know is that extra- virgin olive oil is what I'm supposed to buy, but I don't know why. John chooses a bottle in the mid-price range. Our brains are on overload by now so we grab a loaf of bread from the bakery and move toward the checkout lanes.

The sympathetic cashier who made change for us earlier sits to ring the items. With my long history in retail, I'm shocked that the cashiers are allowed to sit. She looks bored, and when I'm not thinking about her being perched on a stool, I'm gaping at her thick kohl eyeliner. While all this distracts me, she inquires, *"Quante borse?"* Huh? Is she asking us "Paper or plastic?" No, she's asking how any bags and has given up on us understanding and responding to her question. Plastic bags are the only option and cost about a nickel each. She snatches a few bags and tosses them at us. Seeing that everyone else is sacking their own groceries, John and I get busy doing the same. When the cashier starts to scan the produce we hit another snag. We didn't notice we were supposed to weigh the bags and apply price stickers to them. We are not making any friends by holding up the line while I run back to the produce section to do this. It takes a minute or two and I'm sweating and my neck and face are hot when I return.

When we're given the total, the cashier has to repeat the amount at least three times. She has a melodic voice, but as the words roll off her tongue, *"ottanta quattro, quattro cento ottanta,"* *(£84.480)* it sounds like we owe hundreds of thousands of dollars for six bags of groceries. I hand over a fistful of lire and she gives me the change and a receipt large enough to do homework on.

We gather up the bags and head for the exit. With all the

confusion, someone has nabbed our grocery basket. Lesson three: Keep your eyes on your basket or risk losing your deposit.

The walk back home is longer toting heavy bags, and we don't stop to gaze at the mosaics of Santa Maria in Trastevere this time. The importance of a two-wheeled cart has become evident, and we promise to make it our next purchase. But for now, it's time for lunch.

Spaghetti can be eaten most successfully if you inhale it like a vacuum cleaner.

–Sophia Loren

A Home-Cooked Meal

Later that day

John's taking a nap, I'm flipping through *O, The Oprah Magazine,* an artifact of my American lifestyle, and I am only now realizing how wonderfully peaceful it is here. Not in a no-noise, silent way, but peaceful in that the sounds drifting through our apartment windows are gentle and soothing. Rather than distracting me from reading, the sound of scuffling on a patio, plates clinking in a nearby kitchen, the rev of a motorcycle from the *vicolo* and muffled voices from an open window let me know that we are not alone. We're a part of this charming neighborhood.

John's awake now and we're hungry, perhaps because we've caught a whiff of the biscotti one of our neighbors is baking. It's only 5:00 p.m., much too early for true Romans to dine, but I decide to make dinner anyway. Starting with the salad, I rummage through the solitary drawer in the kitchen. The only implement to slice the tomatoes is a thin, red-handled knife. The blade is dull, and it makes a bigger mess than necessary. The plastic cutting board is warped, creating a shallow bowl in the middle. This is fortunate actually because the juice running out of the fruit has somewhere to pool instead of dripping onto the floor. There is no counter space so I balance the board on the oven's burners and manage to hack the tomatoes into pieces. Pulling open a broiler from under the stove, I quickly scrub it clean and prepare the salmon. We'll broil the fillets, but first we've got to figure out how this gas oven works.

The oven's red knob has no words or numbers encircling it to give us a hint as to temperature. John turns the knob back and forth a few times, but it doesn't seem to accomplish anything. Pulling the oven door wide open, John bends down on one knee and puts his head in the oven to take a better look. Coming back out, he says he's located the pilot light and grabs the large box of wooden matches left by a previous tenant on the pantry shelf. John turns the oven on again and shuts the door. We wait a few seconds to let the gas build up, then bending his six-foot frame over the tiny opened door John strikes the match. KABOOM!

I scream as a hot blast of air shoots out of the oven singeing John's eyebrows. It also produces a rumble so loud and forceful I'm sure all the neighbors around us have heard and will come running to make sure we're okay. No one comes. If the neighbors are home and have heard the roar and my screams, they aren't too concerned. Rather, this probably happens each semester as a new student or visiting professor takes this apartment and has to learn the ropes. I imagine the neighbors chuckling and saying to each other, "I guess the *americani* figured it out," and then going on with whatever they were doing.

The salmon is ready for broiling. I rarely cooked fish in Houston due to nearly year-round air conditioning and lack of ventilation. With windows sealed shut, the fishy smell would linger for days, mercilessly reminding me of a meal long past. Here, we can throw the windows wide open and delight in the cross breeze circulating in our *appartamento* on the fourth floor.

In our haste during this morning's grocery shopping, we neglected to pick up a bottle of wine, but a little liquor store on Via della Scala one street over has caught my eye. Leaving John in charge of cooking the salmon, I dash down the stairs, out the front door and up and around the end of our *vicolo* to the wine shop.

Teetering on the paved cobbles sits a small bistro table and two chairs at the entrance to the wine shop. A short, gray-haired woman I've already seen here a day or two ago is sitting in the same chair, talking with a man with gray whiskers in the chair opposite. It seems obvious she is the wife or mother of the shopkeeper, but I don't know why I am so sure of this. She seems completely comfortable, as if she were sitting in her own home.

Inside the small, well-stocked store, hundreds of bottles are on display in dusty, slanted racks and stacked cardboard boxes. A man is pouring wine at another tiny round table inside the store. It appears he is hosting an informal wine tasting. Two men are breathing in the aroma, their Roman noses unpretentiously dipped in the glasses. They take a sip, and, I suppose from the flow of conversation that follows, offer their opinions. I wander up and down the two aisles becoming more confused about the right wine to choose when a man from behind the counter greets me, *"Buona sera, signora."* My heart melts a little.

Carefully, I recite a memorized phrase asking for a recommendation, *"Consiglio una bottiglia per salmone?"*

He responds, *"Certo,"* or "Certainly," and joins me in the aisle. He immediately plucks two bottles from the dusty racks and holds them out for my inspection. I randomly choose one that costs about six dollars. He puts the bottle in a brown paper sack and thanks me. I'm hesitant about leaving the shop; I'd like to hang out here a while longer but my stomach is growling. Besides, I know I'll come back soon and maybe next time the man pouring wine will offer me a taste, too.

It's now about 6:00 p.m. and the streets are getting more populated as people take their *passeggiata* – an afternoon stroll through the piazzas. Almost every person I pass on my way home is eating gelato. How do they stay so slim and why are they eating ice cream right before dinner? But then I remember Italian custom is to dine closer to 9:00 or 10:00 p.m. I walk back up Via della Scala, around the end of the street and hike back up the three flights of stairs. I surmise it is not a problem for Italians to keep weight off with all the walking they do. I hope it won't be a problem for us either. John and I sold our vehicles in Houston and have no plans of buying one here. John is an avid cyclist and amateur racer and is naturally thin, but I will plump up quickly if I don't keep moving.

Back in the kitchen, despite a dangerous start, John has done an excellent job cooking the salmon, drizzling fresh lemon juice over the fillets as a finishing touch. They are just the right shade of pink and the fork test shows them to be flaky but not over cooked. A simple salad of arugula, or rocket, as it is known here, the mangled tomatoes and enormous olives stuffed with almonds are tossed in a blue plastic bowl. Along with the wine, we drink tap water with no ice. The freezer doesn't have an icemaker or ice trays. On previous visits, I'd noticed Italian restaurants do not put ice in water. We make this minor adjustment painlessly.

The layout of this apartment is undeniably strange with the bedroom sandwiched between the living room and the kitchen. There are no chairs and no room to sit down to eat in the kitchen, so we carry dinner plates, beverages and silverware from the kitchen through the boudoir to the table in the living room. Awkward? For sure, but not fatal.We are far more concerned about looking gauche to our neighbors across the courtyard. While we love the view and the ability to observe our Italian neighbors going about their day, it isn't without a catch. Not only can we see them, but they also can see us and we are accustomed to eating dinner early, around 6:30 or 7:00 p.m. We are so hungry, we sheepishly pull in the shutters, blocking their view of us, as we sit down and devour our first home-cooked meal well before the sun has set.

After we clear the table and wash the dishes by hand, it is too quiet with no television or stereo as background noise. We take a walk in search of dessert and find a bakery open on San Francesco a Ripa. John has been a fan of Nutella for years and it is a popular Italian- made product. Standa sells liter-sized jars stacked on an end cap that seem more like promotional props than actual grocery items. Warm pastries with this chocolate hazelnut spread make a perfect after- dinner treat. We buy a couple of them and, still standing in the shop, savor all their gooey goodness.

With sticky hands, we return home. Before even approaching the door to our building we catch a whiff of the unmistakable aroma of garlic and onions sautéing. Clinking pots and lively voices get more distinct as we climb the stairs, passing the apartment where a neighbor is preparing dinner. I wonder what delectable feast is being served tonight. Perhaps sausage with mushrooms. Or if that is too heavy for a warm night, a simple tomato sauce with fresh basil served over homemade ravioli and topped with shaved *parmigiano*. I like the idea of eating dinner late like this. I vow to make this adjustment and live like our fellow Romans even if it means having to eat more gelato.

To every bird, his own nest is beautiful.

—Italian Proverb

Home Improvement

The cloudless blue sky and white stucco facade of Santa Maria della Scala offer a striking view from our bedroom window. Starlings play a game of chase, resting momentarily on the lower cross of the bell tower, then darting down and swooping back up after their prey before resting again on a higher cross atop the angled roof. This is a tranquil moment and one I am not accustomed to, having led a fast- paced life before.

As much as I love the view from our apartment, its practicality is equally enticing. Equidistant between the Coliseum and the Vatican, the location has turned out to be even better than we could have imagined. It takes only five minutes to walk to the university along paved cobbles, where wisteria drape heavily off the rooftops. With a bare-bones gym fewer than one hundred steps from the front door, two movie theaters (one dedicated to English-language movies), a bustling outdoor food market (San Cosimato), a plethora of Catholic churches, lots of shops, including The Almost Corner Bookshop, an English-language bookstore, and plenty of restaurants all within walking distance, we couldn't have picked a better place to live.

9 September 2001

Our classes (John's university, my language school) start next week so we take advantage of this time to get ourselves oriented and to organize our new home.

In Houston, we had a patio besieged with pigeons leaving poop and feathers all around. It was so unpleasant that we rarely sat outside. Finally, the only thing that worked was having a maintenance man install chicken wire the entire length of the wooden railing all the way up to the roof. It wasn't attractive, but the mess and constant warbling were so irritating it was our best option.

Now, here in Rome we face a similar problem. Did they follow us here? Our miniscule bathroom can be a little claustrophobic; we can't open the window because of the familiar cooing on the other side. We decide the pigeons will have to find a new place to roost. Without a maintenance man to complain to, we take it upon ourselves to remedy the situation.

But before we get started – breakfast – a great excuse to stop for a cappuccino on the way to the hardware store. We stop at Checco, a small, narrow bar with a more extensive offering of pastries than the bar on the other end of the street. Coffee shops are called bars as they usually serve alcohol too.

* * *

Italians do not eat big breakfasts. Coffee and a single pastry is the norm. No bacon and eggs or biscuits and sausage. No stacks of pancakes or waffles dripping in syrup. I'm famished but do not want to look gluttonous to the Italian patrons or barista so I order only one buttery *cornetto* and a cappuccino, as does John. I'm still hungry when we leave, but push the feeling aside. It's time to go native. We live here now.

The streets of Trastevere are quiet with many of the shops closed due to *Ferragosto*. This Catholic celebration of the Assumption of the Virgin Mary, observed officially on August 15, has expanded to take over the month of August. In one mass pilgrimage, the city empties out and deposits its inhabitants onto the sandy beaches of the Italian coast. Some businesses close for two or three weeks, others for the entire month.

We're in luck. The hardware store across from Checco is open but it is tiny – barely able to hold three customers at a time. Inventory is stacked from floor to ceiling and the overflow spills outside onto an uneven grassy area where a sidewalk should be. We are specifically looking for some type of material to keep the pigeons from roosting in the "corridor" in our bathroom wall. Not finding anything suitable for this project, we take note of a laundry rack designed to hang from a window ledge. That will come in handy when we start doing our laundry so we'll come back for that, but for now we aim for Viale Trastevere, the main drag.

Window displays of the few shops that are open stop me in my tracks, vying for my attention and tempting me with rich brown leather boots, woven handbags and trendy tops adorned with faux fur trim, and ironically, feathers. John calls me "Swivelhead" because I cannot stop looking. My husband shops like most men: focusing on the task at hand and dismissing everything else. I am like most women, who take a broader view, filing away important details that we may need another day. Who knows when we'll require a white tank top spruced up with camouflage fringe and really holey jeans? To not pay attention would be careless. I have to stop to look, and it's a good thing too because by slowing down at a florist stand, I find the perfect solution to our pigeon problem. Peering past the healthy green plants, I notice the black plastic crates that have transported them thus far appear to fit all of our requirements: sturdy material, latticed bottom allowing air to flow, and, above all, cheap. One of these crates cut down to size would be strong enough to deter the birds but still provide ventilation.

"Quanto costa?" or how much? I ask the shopkeeper pointing to the plastic crate.

"Che?" he replies, looking puzzled. Using my hands as a true Italian would, I try to explain that I don't want the plants that are taking up most of the crate, only the crate. He shrugs, and without further inquiry empties out the potted plants and hands the crate to John, gesturing that we just take it – no charge. To show our appreciation, we purchase an aromatic basil plant that I pray won't meet the fate of my other attempts at container gardening. Besides adding a little life to our new home, the fragrant herb will come in handy for all the new recipes I'm planning to try.

We stop at a bar on Viale Trastevere for lunch on the way home. Freshly baked focaccia with olive oil drizzled over mozzarella and tomato slices has already become my favorite panino or sandwich. John orders his with prosciutto and mozzarella. Asked if we want it *scaldo,* or heated, we nod eagerly. Warming the sandwiches in a panino press takes what is already delicious up several more notches.

John doesn't mention until we arrive home that we have no tools or knives strong or sharp enough to cut the crate. Making do with what we have, he pulls the lone, wimpy, red plastic-handled knife from the single kitchen drawer and turns on the gas stove burner. By repeatedly heating the blade over the open flame, John painstakingly applies it to the crate, slowly cutting and shaping it to fit the window.

As John finishes forming the pigeon barrier, I clean the window ledge's bottom, sides and top thoroughly with soapy water. Then John shoves the plastic screen into place. By cutting it larger than the opening it fits snugly to stand up to persistent pigeons that might knock it in. It works!

Having achieved success with our first home improvement project, we return a few days later to the tiny hardware store to purchase the laundry drying rack. John secures it to the windowsill in the kitchen. We don't have a washing machine yet so we schlep our dirty laundry in a giant, blue IKEA bag down to the corner *lavanderia*. To save money, we lug the clean, wet clothes home and hang them outside on the drying rack. The best part, besides not having to use energy and money to pay to dry them, is the incredible fresh scent. Ah, the simple pleasures.

Oh, but there was one drawback. The pigeons we have evicted earlier aren't too happy about losing their cozy resting place, and they settle the score on our freshly washed laundry more than once.

What we learn only through the ears makes less impression upon our minds than what is presented to the trustworthy eye.
                                                          -Horace, Ancient Roman Poet

First Impressions: Meeting the Neighbors

We haven't seen too many neighbors in our building since our move-in coincided with *Ferragosto*. But this evening a car is parked in front of the double doors, each braced open by a large rock. A family is unloading their car, placing suitcases and various other bags inside the door and on the first few steps. We attempt to introduce ourselves and tell them which apartment we inhabit. A large, motherly figure, Signora Oberti smiles broadly and proudly introduces herself, husband Federico, son Antonio, and adorable grandsons Alonzo and Piero. We can't say much else at this point, but in an attempt to make a good impression, we motion that we will help carry the bags upstairs.

They are all very appreciative, except for Birillo – their very large dog, who decides John, who has picked up some of Federico's belongings, is a threat and lunges at him, baring his teeth, showing his fierceness. The dog's barking is deafening as it echoes through the stairwell. Alonzo and Piero, who are only four and seven-years old respectively, struggle as they pull back on Birillo's leash. Antonio, their father, a tall brawny man, grabs the dog's collar, reprimanding him in Italian, and pulling him back outside. A friendly introduction becomes a chaotic exchange, with them trying to calm Birillo and us jostling bags and navigating the narrow staircase as we continue to help them unload.

It all becomes funny to everyone and we share a laugh - a multi- cultural icebreaker if there ever is one. We feel a kinship with Signora Oberti and her family from that moment on.

I always refer to Signora Oberti formally, though I'm sure she wouldn't mind if I call her by her first name. She is a strong, full-figured woman, very warm and motherly. When she and I speak, I feel more like her daughter than a neighbor. When I become frustrated with the language, she pats my arm and says, *"Piano, piano,"* slowly it will come.

Soon after I get to know Signora Oberti better, she starts pulling me in to their apartment for caffè or lunch. I discover some delicious meals in the warmth of her kitchen. One simple pasta dish of *dittalini* (little thimbles) with tomato sauce is memorable for exactly that reason – it is simple and delicious.

Signora Oberti often sends extra servings home with me for John. I try to reciprocate with homemade chocolate chip cookies, which are not commonly found in Italy. Grocery stores do not stock chocolate chips but I improvise with candy bars; I take them and whack away at them, making "gourmet" chocolate chips.

When we first settle in, we have to make large and small adjustments. Though Rome is a major metropolitan city, life moves at a slower pace than what we are used to. When I run errands, I am either too early or too late for the shops to be open. And then there is getting used to military time. If a business posts that it will re-open at 16:00 that means 4:00 p.m.

I also discover that finding general household items can be challenging. To replace a light bulb, for instance, I have to find a light fixture shop. Once there, I find every type of bulb imaginable, even the kind that fit my Itty Bitty Book Light. There is no superfluous packaging, just the bare bulb, which cost only a few cents. The store employee places the bulb in an itty, bitty paper bag for me.

A few days after arriving in Rome, we need to buy a cell phone for me. John receives one with his paid tuition, the "all-inclusive package" at the university. Buying my cell phone is a rare instance when something is actually simpler than in the United States. We don't have to sign a lengthy, expensive mobile contract. We simply purchase the phone and charge it with prepaid minutes. No bills to worry about, no overspending. *Brilliant!*

Cell phones are ubiquitous, and ironically, their conspicuous use does not bother me as they did in the U.S. Maybe eavesdropping on a beautiful language and not knowing exactly what mundane conversations are taking place make it more enjoyable. We learn how to text messages, which is already popular in Italy but has not caught on in the States yet.

John tells me that we need to register with the American Embassy. In case of an emergency they will have a record of where we live and can get in touch with us. I cannot imagine why that would be necessary; we are living in Italy, not a country associated with upheaval these days, but I don't mind. The American Embassy is near Via Veneto, an area of Rome once depicted years ago in movies—think *Roman Holiday* and *La Dolce Vita*—as the cool place. We arrive at the Embassy, complete the paperwork and are on our way without much ado.

John also suggests that we buy a radio. We find an appliance store on the Lungotevere, a wide road (compared to the many narrow streets) in Trastevere that leads to the Vatican. The store sells everything from refrigerators to alarm clocks. We purchase a small short-wave radio.

We find ourselves slipping into the Italian lifestyle pretty easily. No major culture shock. We have our moments, of course. One especially trying day for example, John loses a bus ticket from his back pocket. No big deal, but then the debit card is misplaced and he thinks he has lost it in the same way. The card is the lifeline to our checking and savings accounts— all the money we have so carefully put aside for this 21-month adventure. We pace back and forth in the weird layout of our tiny *appartamento*, wracking our brains, "Where could the card be? What will we do if all our money has been stolen?' It is a long fifteen minutes until we discover the card safely tucked away with his passport. We realize we are more stressed than we think.

Moving to a new country, quitting our secure jobs, going back to school and being away from our friends, not to mention being a couple of decades older than the average student in our classes, are taking their toll.

We feel old and out of place when on a bus tour of an overview of Rome with other students from the university. They seem as confused as the Italians we've met when we explain that John is a student, not a professor. Here's a typical conversation with an Italian:

Me: "*Mio marito* (husband) *è uno studente.*"
Italian: "*No, no, insegnante,*" a teacher, they correct me.
Me: "*No, no, studente,*" I insist. The conversation goes back and forth and ends with them usually convinced that I don't know what I am talking about.

We don't fit into any typical role they are used to and it makes us feel even more like outsiders.

We begin to pick up on subtle cultural differences:

o   It is perfectly acceptable to walk down the street while eating gelato, but you should not eat pizza this way, even if it is sold by the slice. It is considered gauche to eat anything but gelato walking around and Italians just don't do it.

o   Italians never wear shorts.

o   Italians do wear the same clothing two days in a row. I ask Steven, an American who lived in Germany before moving to Italy, about this habit and am told, "The clothes haven't gotten dirty yet, so it is perfectly acceptable to wear the same outfit on back-to-back days."

○ Italians don't buy special clothing for working out. John and I join a small, no-frills gym about one hundred steps from our front door. Members wear loose-fitting garments, probably something they have owned for a while.

There are other mundane rituals of daily life that become second nature to us, like seeing other people's laundry. It has been said that Trastevere has some of the most photographed laundry lines in the world. Signora Oberti's laundry line squeaks whenever she draws it in, so I know without looking out the window that it's washday for her. I love seeing her colorful sheets and her grandsons' shirts and jeans flapping in the wind.

We are thrilled when the university prods our landlord into buying a washing machine for our apartment. When it arrives, we discover it is the tiniest washing machine we have ever seen; yet it is just perfect for our miniscule home. To our astonishment, it takes over two hours to wash one load! And that is the shortest amount of setting offered by the appliance.

Risparmiare translates to "to save, to spare." We learn how important it is to conserve energy. If I am running a load of wash, I can't use my hair dryer. I keep forgetting and blow the circuit breaker many times. It reminds me of a scene straight out of the sitcom *Green Acres*. When this happens, one of us must descend to the first floor and flip the switch in the breaker box to get the electricity flowing again. Fortunately, my absent mindedness doesn't affect our neighbors.

Another surprising difference is how casually Italians litter. You regularly see them unwrap a pack of cigarettes, drop the cellophane to the ground and continue walking. Littering is not such a terrible thing? "Someone is getting a job from cleaning it up. And they do keep the streets clean," according to Iris, a Trastevere shopkeeper. On the mornings I rise for an early run, I am shocked to see beer bottles, cans and papers strewn around the fountain in Piazza Santa Maria in Trastevere. A garbage truck vacuums up the debris (even bottles and cans), sprays water, and with round, rotating brushes scrubs the area clean. Another component of Trastevere is what many would refer to as bums, who all seem to own dogs. *Punkabbestia* is the Italian name for these fascinating street dwellers, heavily pierced and donning black garb from head to toe. They hang out with their pooches on the Ponte Sisto foot bridge or choose a spot in a piazza and offer up a tin cup, or more often than not, a paper cup from McDonald's, for anyone willing to spare a few coins. My personal policy is never to give them money. Since this is where I live, I don't want to get solicited every time I pass by. But that policy does not seem to matter as they don't discriminate and I am always asked anyway. They are never threatening, and they don't seem offended when I just smile, shake my head and keep walking.

Other patterns in our Roman lifestyle emerged. If it's Thursday, it must be *gnocchi*. That's the day the shops that sell hand-made *gnocchi* open. These potato-based pastas are so delicious and affordable I would never try to make them myself. Just tell the seller how many people will be dining and they'll determine how much is needed. They will expertly wrap the order in butcher paper, and carefully tie it with a string—a beautiful package to take home to cook that night. Done!

I learn Trastevere's outdoor market, San Cosimato has fresh fish for sale on Tuesdays and Fridays. One time, I bought fresh spinach at the market at Campo de' Fiori and thought I'd been given enough to feed the entire neighborhood. After I told the vendor I needed enough for two people (*per due persone*), she stuffed so much spinach in the bag that I was convinced she was taking me to the bank. I tried stopping her, but she kept shoving more greens into the bag. Once I started cooking the spinach, however, with a little garlic and olive oil on my little gas burner in my compact kitchen, I understood why she had given me so much. The spinach started shrinking and by the time I was done cooking, I had almost nothing left! It was like the great disappearing greens magic trick. I still feel bad for thinking ill of the woman who sold it to me.

The *arrotino* is an interesting character that appears in Trastevere on Fridays. His livelihood is sharpening knives and he arrives on his specially built, motorized bicycle equipped with sharpening tools. His distinctive bellow carries through the open windows as he announces himself by hollering "*ARROTINO, ARROTINOOOO.*" The building's tenants in need of his services then lower a basket from their window with cutlery in need of honing.

Saturdays almost always mean a wedding or two. A Rome-based wedding planner teaches me that tradition dictates that all guests and members of the wedding party must wait outside the church to witness the bride's arrival. It is a special moment that no Italian wants to miss.

The first time I walk through Piazza Sant'Egidio in my workout gear— running top, nylon shorts and running shoes— I feel very much an alien, and not just a foreigner but like an alien from outer space. I am on my way to the tree-shaded steps leading to Monte Gianicolo and I sense disapproval from the people I meet; a grandmotherly type and a pair of *carabineri* (policemen), in their early twenties, share a knowing look of *pazza americana*, or crazy American. I feel their eyes compelling me to slow down and enjoy life.

After the trek through Piazza Sant'Egidio, I have to remember my way up the curvy path between buildings and streets to find the stone and concrete stairs to Monte Gianicolo. On the way, I'll pass the church of San Pietro in Montorio, which is built on the site where Saint Peter is believed to have been crucified. It is also famous for its cloisters and artwork, including Bramante's *Tempietto*. A bit farther uphill is Fontana dell Acqua Paola, a grandiose fountain dating to 1612. You won't see the crowds found at Trevi fountain, but more likely a shimmering white limousine or black Rolls Royce pulling up and an elegantly dressed bride and groom emerging for a photo op. This is a gorgeous setting on its own, and besides being romantic and more private, it also has a domed vista that Trevi doesn't offer. On most days, Palazzo Venezia and Castel Sant'Angelo are easily visible. On a clear day at the right time of year, Colli Albani, the sometimes-snowcapped hills southeast of Rome are visible.

I tell myself to stay on course and keep going because Villa Pamphili, Rome's largest park, is worth the effort it takes to get there. Void of tourists, this running, walking and biking trail draws true Romans. I love watching grandparents pushing strollers during the week with adorably dressed wee ones peering out from cute bonnets or caps. On weekends, couples sensuously embrace each other on grassy areas, and families arrive to picnic and exuberantly cheer soccer games. There is so much life here, with Italians enjoying themselves and each other.

A drinking fountain on the rocky drive to the entrance of Villa Pamphili flows continuously, as do most drinking fountains in Rome. It is clean and safe to drink unless posted signs say otherwise. By watching the locals, I learn how to place my finger over the waterspout to redirect the flow to the small hole on top. This creates a mini geyser from which to drink.

Once, I observe a toddler boy lifted by his father slurping water from the fountain. He drinks and drinks and drinks. When his father pulls him away from the stream of water, the little boy protests, "*Ancora,*" or "Again" in what seems a deep voice for a child. His father relents and allows him to drink until he is sated. Little moments like this allow me to learn bits of the language that really stick. And what a great visual, A*ncora*: again, more, continue. Got it!

What a difference from my usual runs in Houston! There, I would *drive* my car the two miles or so to Memorial Park, praying for a parallel parking spot that isn't too difficult to maneuver. Or after work, I'd *drive* to Rice Stadium and run on the dirt path surrounding it. Here my legs are already a bit fatigued from the steep twenty-minute walk to the park. Now I ease into my jogging pace and hope not to trip on the uneven terrain. There are a few other runners, but mostly walkers, many with dogs and a few mountain bikers.

Another mark of being in Trastevere is the resounding boom of the cannon on Monte Gianicolo every day at noon. It is a bit unsettling at first, but we grow so accustomed to it over time that it feels like an old friend shouting out a greeting. Its reliability—you can set your clock by it—is apparently the reason this ritual was started: to set all the church bells so they all ring at the same time.

John and I get in the habit of going to Mass on Saturday

evenings at Santa Dorotea, a small church down the *vicolo*. We love seeing movies so after attending Mass, we stop along the route for a few slices of pizza or a panino, and then head to the English movie theater in Piazza Sant'Egidio. We attend a few Italian language movies there and earnestly try to understand the dialogue, but our command of the language is such that after a while we settle into not trying to translate every word.

Shopping and navigating through a regular day proves to be mentally exhausting, as I am constantly trying to translate in my head from English to Italian and vice versa, and not just in my Italian classes but all day long with every interaction. It is nice to simply settle into our seats and relax in the darkness of the theater.

This Piazza Sant'Egidio theater, our neighborhood favorite, is a throwback to a simpler time. Always midway through the movie, the lights come up in the theater for an intermission, and employees walk the aisles with strapped-on trays of popcorn and candy to sell. All Rome theaters aren't like this though.

A megaplex in Piazza Barberini is ultramodern. While standing in line to buy our tickets for a Hobbit movie, we can monitor how many seats are still unoccupied on a screen posted above the box office. As we jostle in line with some Italian Hobbit fans, we sweat it out to see if we are going to make the cut. We do, barely. The tickets here also have seat assignments, something we've never encountered in U.S. movie theaters.

A different language is a different vision of life.

—Federico Fellini

Italian Lessons

Enrolled at an intensive language school, my classes will run from nine to noon, Monday through Friday. For the first hour and a half we will focus on grammar, and the last half we'll spend practicing conversation.

I am chomping at the bit to get started. Since learning Italian is all I am going to be doing for a while, I see it as my full-time job. I think once I become semi-fluent I can find a job of some sort. Confident that I can catch on quickly, I intend to be a model student, even more so because I have already prepaid for sixteen weeks of classes.

On my first day of school, I arrive a few minutes early with a flurry of butterflies in my stomach. Some things you never outgrow. The school is near a clock tower where some students are already conversing and smoking one last cigarette before the bell rings.

I wind up the circular marble stairs with the others, find my classroom, and take a seat. The first thing we do is introduce ourselves to each other in Italian and announce where we are from. Then we start. We cover everything I learned the summer before (six weeks at continuing education night school) in the first hour! I am thrilled to be getting started, but simultaneously apprehensive about keeping up. I am determined though to learn the language and speak it well.

After an hour and a half, we take a break and switch classes. The teacher for conversation could have been a doppelganger for Tracy Ullman. She not only looks just like her, but she is also funny like her too. *Thank goodness for that.* Laughter is a great stress reliever.

Italian immersion should have been named submersion—I feel like I am drowning. The classes are completely in Italian; I am not even allowed to ask questions in English, which makes it pretty much impossible for me. Utilizing gestures as much as possible, my attempt at the language looks more like a lesson in charades. I leave each class relieved it is over and vowing to study even harder before the next class. *I can do this; I just know I can,* I tell myself. But it is far more difficult for me than I have imagined. The other students don't seem nearly as stressed.

I start dreading class, despite loving the walk to school. Each morning I take a left out the door of Vicolo del Bologna 15 and follow the cobbles to the Tiber, continuing across the Ponte Sisto footbridge, which is popular with artists. They often set up their canvases and paint scenes of the Vatican dome in the distance. With reflections on the water of the Garibaldi and Mazzini bridges on either side, I almost have to pinch myself that this isn't a dream. *I am so incredibly lucky to see this beauty every morning,* I muse.

Always nervous about class, I often repeat phrases or conjugate verbs as I amble along. The twenty-minute jaunt to school could easily run longer if I allow myself to get distracted when passing through Campo de' Fiori. The colorful vegetable, fruit, flower and fish market in this most popular of piazzas draws both locals and tourists. Souvenir t- shirts, aprons and knick-knacks are also for sale. A bronze statue of Giordano Bruno, a philosopher who was burned to death for heresy in this same spot, is a convenient meeting place for party-goers — as it is hard to miss. At night, wine bars and restaurants fill up and the music plays until all hours. But early morning is still my favorite time of day to be here. The aroma of espresso from coffee bars and freshly baked bread from Antico Forno Roscioli, one of the most revered bakeries in Rome, is intoxicating.

Once I pass through Campo de' Fiori, I still have other hurdles to making it to school on time -- newsstands. They are everywhere in Rome. I've always been drawn to magazine racks like a moth to a flame. I find it nearly impossible not to stop and linger for at least a few minutes. I am constantly searching for publications in English, a guilty pleasure for John and me. *The International Herald Tribune* is the one English-language newspaper we can count on every day. *The New York Times* Sunday edition arrives later in the week, but by that time, we usually have read the main stories on the Internet at the university or at an Internet cafe (no connection at home) and cannot justify the expense. Missing my monthly fix of *O, The Oprah Magazine,* one morning I ask the *giornalaia,* or news seller, if she carries it. She smiles broadly and seems impressed as she nods, "*Oh, sì!*" Then she happily hands me a magazine titled *Opera*!

I often promise to allow myself more time after class to browse before tearing myself away from the newsstands, only to be faced with another serious distraction: store windows. Retailers present their most fabulous merchandise in an attempt to draw in passersby like me. It works beautifully. Another nice feature that you don't see in shops in the U.S. is the detailed "laundry list" of prices for all the items on display. It makes sense to have these lists in the windows so that before you rush in ready to buy that "must have" handbag, you aren't disappointed and embarrassed to find that it is *molto caro*, or very expensive, and, as in my case, completely out of my price range.

Once at school, I enjoy the grammar lessons because of the structure. I always do my homework, and as long as we are doing the exercises in the book I can keep up. When the teacher ventures off on a tangent, always speaking in Italian, so I have no idea what she is saying—I start to zone out. I fixate on any word that sounds remotely like English and try to compose a sentence around that vaguely familiar word. I'm sure this method is not a recommended tip in any language book. I do learn to try not to look too confused because that seems to draw unwanted attention. I pretend to understand and imitate my fellow students as much as possible.

We are well into the second week of classes before I comprehend the reference to *essercheetzee*. The teacher has spoken this word many times, and I have never had any idea what she is referring to. Then one day, like Helen Keller at the water pump, the word finally clicks in my brain when everyone in the class opens their book after she says, "essercheetzee." Ah, the exercises! *Esercizi!* We are going over the exercises! *A breakthrough! I'm pathetic.*

For the first few weeks, I am barely hanging on. Barely. We are speaking baby talk, learning colors and numbers and describing our homes, our friends and family, and really just memorizing nouns.

I can do this, I tell myself, not entirely sure I can.

A warm smile is the universal language of kindness.
                                    –William Arthur Ward

9/11

It was obvious that moving abroad would be life changing for us, but we didn't know how much life back in the States would be changing, too. I attended my second day of intensive Italian classes on the morning of September 11, 2001. As I walked home afterwards, I overhear two American study-abroad students talking.

"It would be so easy to hijack a plane," one of them says. That registers as an odd thing to be discussing, but I dismiss it almost immediately.

John is studying at the living room table as I open our apartment door. Simultaneously, the only other American who lives in our building shows up at our door. Visibly upset, Terri asks us, "Have you guys heard? The U.S. is under attack." Terri's mother, who lives in Los Angeles has just called to tell her that some airplanes have been hijacked and two have crashed into the World Trade Center.

My first thought is disbelief. *No way could this be true.* We don't own a television and have only purchased a radio a few days before. We turn the radio on and begin hearing confirmation of what Terri has just relayed.

After a little while, John leaves to go to his afternoon class, but returns almost immediately—all classes have been cancelled for the rest of the day and the next. John and I spend the next several hours listening intently to the BBC on our shortwave radio. When we venture out into the neighborhood hours later, it is eerily quiet. Almost no one is out for *passeggiata*, and those we do see are somber.

We are stunned by the news, but it is surreal. We lack the constant barrage of video and news reports everyone else is monitoring. Our limited language skills prevent us from talking to other people to get their perspective on the event.

The next day, I attend Italian class more for an opportunity to be with other people than for the lesson itself. While the class consists of an international mix of students (Japanese, Swedish, Danes and Germans), most are from the United States. Our teacher, Stefania, makes an exception to her personal policy of never speaking English to us. She asks us to talk about the previous day's events as a way of dealing with the grief.

One classmate, Diana, is a fifty-something New Yorker who is learning Italian so she can communicate with the workers who are renovating a house she has purchased south of Naples, *a la "Under the Tuscan Sun."* She sadly tells us she has many friends and business associates who work in the World Trade Center. Steven, who has also lived in Germany, a gifted twenty-seven-year old linguist who is learning Italian as his eighth language, recalls that he gave tours of the World Trade

Center as a teenager. Another student, a thirty-year-old, former equestrian champion from D.C. expresses concern about his mother because of the hijacking of the plane meant to strike the Pentagon.

I listen as the Americans continue to relate stories of their friends, family members and colleagues who live or work in the areas that have been attacked. I am impressed by our instructor and by the other foreign students in the class. They are as upset as any of the Americans, and they share with us their lifelong plans to visit the U.S. someday. They speak with reverence and respect for our country. And they all speak English fluently. I begin to understand how the United States looks to those living outside of it. Even though this is only the third day of classes, my classmates and I bond quickly.

We share a long moment of silence for the tragedy before class begins. I head home after class, but decide to stop at my neighborhood outdoor market to pick up some fresh produce. As I admire the gorgeous bounty at one stand, the vendor asks if I am American. When I respond with a nod, he lowers his voice and his words are sympathetic. I feel enveloped in a cross-cultural hug and finally begin to cry. Though I don't understand exactly what he is saying, I know what he means, sensing the deep feeling behind his words. From that day on, I always shop with Alberto and his lovely wife, Bruna.

That evening, John and I have dinner with Natalie, a new friend from San Francisco. She has just arrived in Rome to work at the university for a year. As we dine *al fresco* at a charming *trattoria* with red-checkered tablecloths, the horrors of 9/11 seem unimaginable. I feel guilty for being here while everyone back home is dealing with such incredible stress.

The U.S. Embassy begins sending e-mail messages every few days. The messages warn Americans to "limit movement," and to stay away from "symbols of American capitalism." We take that to mean eating at McDonald's and not that we went there very often, sometimes it did feel good to stop by for something familiar, "Quarter Pounder with cheese, please." As much as possible, we avoid the main tourist destinations and American fast food restaurants. We feel safe tucked away in this little Roman neighborhood.

On my return home from errands a couple of days later, I find our next-door-neighbor, a slim, white-haired man with a kind face leaning against the building. Wearing what I would eventually come to recognize as his signature outfit, an argyle cardigan layered over a checked shirt and corduroy trousers, he is smoking a cigarette. He speaks no English, but expresses his sadness in true Italian style, using his hands, which are suntanned and wrinkled, to describe the impact.

On the Sunday following the attacks, Santa Susanna, the American Church of Rome, holds a special memorial service. We meet up with Natalie and take a taxi there arriving just as Mass begins. It is standing room only, despite the embassy's warning to stay away from areas where Americans congregate. Two twenty- something men have literally wrapped themselves in American flags, the pain of the last few days evident on their faces.

The ambassador to the Holy See is scheduled to speak. His carefully worded speech doesn't touch on any real emotion regarding what has happened and does little to make us feel better.

* * *

16 September 2001

I went for a run in Villa Pamphili, this afternoon, the beautiful park atop the hill from Trastevere. It was a wholly different place than last Sunday. Every person, whether sitting on a park bench or on the grass with family members or reclining against a tree, was reading a newspaper. There were no soccer games like last weekend and only solemn faces on those I met on the trail. It was a beautiful day, but the crisp air was silent. The only sound I heard was of my shoes crunching the gravel, and it seemed obnoxious. I decided to walk instead of run and considered tiptoeing so as not to disturb anyone.

Rome had been bustling again after *Ferragosto*. Tourists had arrived and businesses were open once more, bringing the city back to life. But after 9/11, it all quiets down again. The impact on the U.S., of course, is affecting the Italian economy as well. Some people change their plans to study abroad after 9/11.

I ran into Kathryn, one of the young women in my language class, near Torre Argentina. We went to a caffé for gelato, where she confides she's cutting her Italian stay short. Having recently graduated from college, she originally planned to live in Rome for at least six months. Besides attending language classes, she's working as an au pair and is making around $15 an hour, but understandably she wants to be close to her family right now.

I do my best to convince her to stay; she is by far one of the best students in the class, having studied Spanish for several years. I don't want to see her lose this opportunity, but she has made up her mind and will return to Oregon at the end of our four-week session.

* * *

When John and I made our budget for living in Rome, we didn't include trips back to the States, planning instead to spend any extra money we might have traveling around the Continent. We weren't worried about getting homesick; our friends and family were going to be visiting us. But after 9/11, all their plans change.

Later that week, John and I take a bus from Trastevere across the Tiber at Ponte Garibaldi to Piazza Popolo and walk to the Spanish Steps.

Our route takes us past enormous royal blue billboards with yellow block letters stating support for the United States and no tolerance for *"terrorismo."* My heart swells, and I fight back tears seeing this bold outpouring of compassion.

Being warned to stay away from tourist spots by the U.S. Embassy, my interest in what people are wearing goes beyond my curiosity in fashion as I do double takes at anyone toting a backpack. As we wend our way through the streets, I cannot help but imagine being blown to bits while walking through Piazza di Spagna near the Spanish Steps, but John needs to purchase textbooks at a bookstore a few streets over so we press on. My thoughts are quite a contrast to two weeks ago when my biggest concern was paying inflated prices for gelato and bottled water in a tourist must-see area.

A few weeks later we have settled back into a routine. School is going well for John and I am trying to be the best Italian student I can be. We shop for food at Standa and the local *mercato*. One day, as I look over the enormous lemons available at the produce stand of Alberto and Bruna, another American woman walks up. Alberto feels compelled to introduce us. He points to me and says, "*Lei, americana,*" Then points to the other woman and says, "*Lei, americana.*" He moves his hands back and forth, gesturing for us to get together and meet each other.

Sherry and I hit it off immediately. Her husband is employed by the State Department and is working on projects at the American Embassy in Rome. We liv e within blocks of each other, and Sherry and I began to meet regularly at a *caffé* becoming fast friends.

A few weeks later, we bring our husbands along and meet for dinner at John's favorite hole-in-the-wall restaurant. The menu is posted only outside and Sherry and I order ravioli. When John and Marty don't decide quickly enough, the diminutive waiter with coke-bottle glasses points to each of them, saying, "*bucatini,*" "*bucatini,*" and scribbles it down on his tablet. Whether they like it or not (and they did, of course) John and Marty are to dine on thick spaghetti with tomato and meat sauce. And that was that.

Women dress alike all over the world: they dress to be annoying to other women.
    −Elsa Schiaparelli, Italian-born French Fashion Designer

Recipe For Italian Dressing

In a country where Armani designs the police uniforms, it isn't surprising that women take dressing seriously. Italian women take great pride in putting themselves together, as I mentioned earlier, this is known as the *bella figura*. After getting the rudimentary necessities to set up our home, I quickly become obsessed with emulating the fashionable style of Italian women or *donne*.

Never wanting to be taken for a tourist, I desperately want to blend in. I know I don't have "the look" and am not even close to it, so I begin studying what Roman women are wearing. I conclude that Italian dressing requires not blending in at all. Showing off one's best assets is the key ingredient, so to blend in you must strive to stand out.

Simona, a friend who runs a *pensione,* a bed and

breakfast, with her family, has noted my growing obsession with Italian fashion and offers this explanation: "Italian women love to look sexy, and it is very important for men to notice them on the street." Simona goes on to clarify that this doesn't mean overt bareness. No, Italian women exude a more subtle sexiness by keeping their bodies fit and wearing slim-cut clothing.

Since arriving, I've been wearing mostly clunky hiking boots with jeans, simple t-shirts and minimal accessories. Cobblestones are tough to walk on in sandals and then there's the *caca* to contend with. Laws to pick up after your pooch are widely ignored so sidewalks and alleys must be navigated much like an obstacle course. One careless step and "slurch," the term John adopts to describe the unfortunate, uncoordinated slip and lurch that takes place upon inadvertently stepping in a pile of dog poop.

Women I want to imitate wear very pointy, high-heeled shoes that look extremely painful. Impressed by how elegantly they walk, not wincing, not complaining and seemingly not watching where they step, I know this isn't going to work for me. My feet have been too spoiled by flats and running shoes, and I am now walking miles and miles every day. I give credit to these women who sacrifice comfort for beauty, but in my heart (and my soles) I know I will not be adapting fully to this look, at least not yet.

Instead, I settle on a pair of black patent oxfords that offer little in the way of style but are less masculine than hiking boots and make me feel less like a dork. I found them at a bargain shoe outlet on Vicolo del Cinque, one street over from our apartment. The shop named Jacques Calzature, is a great find as the shoes they carry have been worn only in fashion shows or photo shoots. I love the simple pricing strategy too—every pair is 50,000 lire, or about $25.

In mid-September, a cold front moves into Rome, which is quite unusual for this time of year. As I trek across the Ponte Sisto on my way to Italian class, wearing jeans, a tank top and a thin pink cardigan, the cold wind coming over the Tiber chills me to the bone. It seems that every man, woman and child I encounter is wearing multiple layers of clothing topped with toasty outerwear, often a quilted jacket and a colorful scarf stylishly wrapped around their necks. I feel more foolish with every freezing step I take and vow that as soon as classes end today I am going to treat myself to something new and more suitable to wear.

I'm so excited about the upcoming shopping trip I find it harder than usual to concentrate on the day's lessons. The dank marble building does little to ward off the chill, and all I can think about is getting warm again. When the bell rings, I make a beeline for the shops in Campo de' Fiori.

The first thing I decide on is a fantastic, black Lycra turtleneck. The slim cut is form fitting, and certainly snugger than my usual roomy tops, but it feels so good to have something covering my chilled body I don't mind. Then one of the two saleswomen shows me a black, chunky-ribbed, shawl collar cardigan with a feature I have never seen before – double zippers. The sweater can be zipped from the top or the bottom, or both, making it cute, cute, cute! The saleswomen are so enthusiastic telling me how great I look, *"Molto bella!"* I start thinking of them as my new lifelong friends. Not only do I buy the pieces they have shown me, but also every word they have uttered.

My two new "friends," *mi amici italiani,* encourage me to wear my new purchases right away and cut the tags off as I gleefully hand over my American Express card. This is the most satisfying shopping experience I have ever had. I immediately feel warm, cozy, and best of all, Italian!

By the third week of Italian classes, I realize I am in serious trouble. Everyone else in class is fluent in at least one other language, which makes a huge difference. Many have also hired tutors.

At the end of the first month of classes, I find myself sitting in the equivalent of the head mistress's office. The next session is starting, which means new teachers and new students. She strongly suggests that I retake some classes, and I know it's for the best but I desperately want to stay in the class with my friend from Chicago, Steven, the brilliant linguist. He senses my frustration and kindly offers to tutor me. I appreciate his offer but know that's too much to ask. Besides, I'm embarrassed. I'll get new teachers, start back at the beginning, and keep trying.

My new *insegnante* (instructor) Rosanna is so upbeat. I begin to enjoy Italian classes again. She yells, *"Brava! Brava! Molto Brava!!"* whenever I say something right. And I love the students in this class too. Rosanna gives us nicknames. She calls the four Swedish soccer players Back Street Boyzzz. *Giornalista* is a television producer from London whose most recent accomplishment is the original *Survivor* show.

I become *Sportiva,* because whenever she asks what I have done the day before I always reply, *"Sono andata in palestra,"* which translates to, "I went to the gym." It's the only thing I can remember how to say.

Conversation class remains painful, but this time around it is full of characters I never want to forget. Like Rosanna, I make up my own nicknames.

Anna Nicole – Suniva (pronounced Sue neeva). From Sweden. Looks just like Anna Nicole Smith. Dresses to attract attention. Probably the best in the class with language and conversational skills.

ToNY – Thirty-something from New York City. Just hanging out having a good time. Says he'd start another career, but he hasn't really had a first one.

Constantine – Tortured German poet. So nice and fun the first day I partnered with him. Distant and moody since. Always flushed. Has the ruffled look down.

Rock Star – Cute, young, from Belgium. Cross between John Mellancamp and Jon Bon Jovi. Scary piercing through his right eyebrow. Never brought his book, pen or paper to class but gets by with a killer smile. Never saw him again after the first week.

Mona Lisa – Spitting image, the portrait come to life. She's an aspiring actress and comes to class maybe every other day.

The Model – Tall, pretty, slender, nice dresser. Has some language skills but speaks with a baby voice.

Boston – Just graduated, seems serious about learning and gets it pretty fast. She reminds me of myself when she can't help asking questions in English.

Olivia Newton John – Joined the class last week. She's too cute – wears very cute clothes. She seems to understand everything.

Tedesco – Big German guy that works hard, does his homework (which it seems no one else does) and turns red all the time. Must be very shy.

Boy from Brazil – Teenager, cute, smart, orthodontia. Only comes to conversation. Gets picked up by a driver in a Mercedes.

Despite the colorful cast, I inevitably start to dread class and even ditch a couple of sessions closer to Christmas. Somehow, shopping for a warm pink scarf to keep the chill off seems like a better use of my time.

I am very busy because I have many things to do.
                            —Gabrielle, the Aristocrat

The Aristocrats

My first brush with royalty occurred one year before John and I moved to Italy, but I hadn't realized it yet. I was in the elevator of the Houston mid-rise where I lived before John and I got married. A woman had just returned from shopping and was struggling with her purchases, which included some gorgeous and fragrant tiger lilies. I stepped in for the ride up. Her blonde hair was cut in a stylish bob. She had on a pink and white-checked shirt left untucked over white jeans, and she wore white cotton gloves, "to protect my hands," she explained. She reminded me of Grace Kelly. She exuded class, but was still approachable. Before the elevator reached our floor, I had learned that she was French, married to an Italian and lived in Rome. I shared with her my dream of living in Italy. When the elevator doors opened again, Gabrielle drew me down the hall to her daughter's apartment.

Inside, we chatted and Gabrielle showed me around the

apartment, which was twice the size of mine. On a wall was a photo of her daughter as a young girl receiving her First Communion, which wasn't that unusual. What made me do a double take was the officiating priest in the photo: Pope John Paul II!

We chatted a little more and exchanged phone numbers. Gabrielle and I saw each other a few times while she was in Houston visiting her daughter. One night she suggested we go to the Italian Cultural and Community Center where you can take, among other offerings, Italian language lessons and cooking classes. Gabrielle insisted on driving and agreeing to this was a mistake on my part. She was a terrible driver! I didn't know it at the time, but all her years of driving in Rome traffic were showing.

It has been at least a year since I last saw Gabrielle. With us back in the same city again, this time Rome, I give her a call after letting several weeks in the Eternal City go by. We make plans to meet a few days later at the non-profit organization where she does volunteer work.

Arriving on foot at the gated entrance, I have to be buzzed in. I'm nervous and excited, and just like at a drive-thru window, have no idea what the person on the intercom has just said to me. I shout Gabrielle's name into the speaker and hope she can hear me. A few minutes later, the gate slowly opens and I see Gabrielle emerge from a doorway in the accompanying courtyard. "Martha!" she calls to me in her charming French accent, holding her arms out to embrace me. Gabrielle pulls me into the office and introduces me to two other volunteers as *"la mia amica americana,"* and then we head to a nearby bar to have coffee and catch up.

The barista smiles and nods to Gabrielle in such a way that I assume she is a regular patron. We sip our *cappuccini* standing at the bar. I attempt to take care of the bill, but Gabrielle waves her hand and says, "I never pay. You will never pay when you're with me." Lesson #1 of life as an aristocrat: What rich people can easily afford, they receive for free.

When we go back to the office, Gabrielle encourages me to stay while she finishes up some things. I chat with Chiara, an Italian who speaks perfect English with a British accent. She tutors students in Italian and lets me practice on her. Gabrielle interrupts us to tell me, "You should be a volunteer." She isn't really asking; her tone indicates that she has already made up her mind and that she is merely letting me know. I agree, of course. I love volunteering and to refuse would be an offense.

A few weeks later Gabrielle invites John and me to her country club for Sunday lunch. The club, built in the 1950s or 1960s, appears pretty traditional and easily fits the stereotype from that era, at least based on what I've seen in movies. There is a swimming pool and tennis courts and the tennis players wear crisp-white outfits.

It's a cloudless autumn day and we'll be having lunch al fresco. A bountiful array of Italian gourmet fare awaits buffet-style beneath tents on the grounds. Gabrielle lets us know her husband, who could not make it today because he is working, will be paying and to have whatever we want. John and I try not to be gluttonous but our plates fill quickly with dishes we have never tried: tortellini stuffed with parsley and ricotta, baked *crespelle* (crepes) with spinach, prosciutto and parmesan filling, risotto with asparagus, baked polenta with Bolognese meat sauce, beef pot roast braised in red wine. We go back for egg custard and Italian chocolate mousse. These new dishes are expertly prepared, making me wish we could spread this feast out over a week's time.

Gabrielle chooses a linen-covered table under the shade of the tent and John and I join her. As Gabrielle's friends or acquaintances stop by our table, Gabrielle again proudly introduces us as *"i miei amici americani."* It seems to give her great pleasure to show she has American friends. Maybe this has something to do with 9/11 so fresh in everyone's mind.

During the course of the meal, where John and I stuff ourselves silly, Gabrielle tells us in her straightforward way, "The people here are very nice; you should become members." She seems shocked when we don't jump at the chance. As flattering as this invitation is, I imagine the membership fees alone would wipe out our entire 21-Month-Plan budget. She apparently has no idea that we saved this money ourselves over years and aren't moneyed *"amici americani."*

At the end of the meal, Gabrielle pulls an elegantly wrapped box from her chic bag and places it in front of me. I will find that each time I am with Gabrielle, she is carrying a different designer handbag —a Ferragamo Kelly bag, Louis Vuitton monogrammed shoulder bag and the like—and today, with her chestnut brown leather Tod's tote, is no different. Inside the beautiful box is a silver sheaf of wheat. I've never seen anything like it. Gabrielle says it represents, *"Tante belle cose,"* all the best and most beautiful things always.

I like the sentiment, but I'm not accustomed to this way of thinking. I admire and enjoy nice things, but don't feel required to own them. But then hanging around with Gabrielle and her friends makes me think why not? Why shouldn't we aspire to only the best in life? It would be easy to get caught up in keeping up with the Missonis, but that would make me miserable. It's a never-ending cycle. I appreciate the gift—it is beautiful—but it's most meaningful because it is from Gabrielle.

A few weeks later, Gabrielle invites me to have lunch at her "club" with her and her friend Katharina, and to later attend *Bolero da Ravel*, a ballet at Teatro Olimpico. After another luscious buffet lunch during our girls-only get-together, Gabrielle presents Katharina and me with another elegantly wrapped present. We find matching black bead bracelets inside, identical to the one Gabrielle is already wearing. Her gesture is reminiscent of exchanging friendship bracelets in grade school; Katharina and I put them on immediately.

We have hours to kill before the ballet. I suggest we go window shopping or walking around the city, but Gabrielle and Katharina seem perfectly content to lounge around the club's heavily decorated living room. I listen to a story about how Katharina and her daughter had an argument about her daughter spending too much money for an item of clothing, a shirt from, "Top Shop or something," she says, her voice trailing off. The amount her daughter has spent is around $250, and Katharina isn't as upset over the amount spent as she is about the shirt's brand, which is one she's never heard of.

Gabrielle turns to me and says, "We don't believe in poofing away money." That is comforting. It's nice to know the rich have rules about spending money. I try to imagine what it would be like to walk in their well-heeled shoes.

* * *

Katharina fascinates me. I've seen her now on several occasions, and she is always impeccably dressed. Today she is wearing a gray flannel wrap skirt and jacket layered over a butter-yellow sweater. The pick stitch detailing and cut of the gray suit make it fresh and modern, but not trendy. Her accessories, supple leather gloves and a leather designer handbag (anyone's guess because there are no obvious initials to give a branding clue) are not boring, basic colors that would "go with everything," but butter yellow, which complements her outfit perfectly. She looks incredibly put together and appears completely comfortable, if not a little bored.

Over the course of the afternoon, Gabrielle, Katharina and I discuss many subjects — books, politics, history,--but never other people (except for their children). They do not dish about their friends or even celebrities. I ask Gabrielle how long she and Katharina have known each other. As soon as the words leave my mouth, I realize I have said something wrong. Gabrielle's face contorts and she sucks in a breath. Uh oh, here it comes.

"That is a rude question! You shouldn't ask such a thing," she admonishes me. I'm baffled at my *faux pas* and immediately ask for an explanation.

"My family and Katharina's family have known each other for hundreds of years so we have always known each other. We have never not known each other."

Okay, okay! I didn't mean to offend, but find this information eye opening.

After that bit of excitement, the afternoon continues to drag on as we while away the hours until the ballet. It's time to stir the pot again. Katharina, who is married to an Italian who always seems to be on a "wild boar hunt," is talking about her home country of Austria. Jokingly, I ask her, "Are you a countess?" Without skipping a beat, she replies, "No, a marquise."

"Huh? " I respond.

She explains, "Gabrielle and I are both marquises. We are equal." "Uh, huh?"

Gabrielle who has been listening to this exchange from a striped armchair, exasperatedly joins the conversation, saying to me, "Don't they teach you anything in school?"

She then sits up from her relaxed pose and removes a pad of paper and pen from her embossed, lipstick-red Kelly bag. She begins writing and then hands me the paper. In two columns, she has listed the hierarchy as follows:

King – Queen
Prince – Princess
Marquis – Marquise
Count – Countess
Baron – Baronne
Sir – Chevalier

I appreciate the tutorial and the first thing that comes to mind pops out of my mouth, "The only thing we have close to royalty in the United States are the Kennedys." Gabrielle huffs, tosses her hand away, and says, "That means nothing."

When we are finally ready to leave for the ballet, Gabrielle tells me we will be picking up another friend of theirs on the way, a princess. I know enough now not to ask too many questions and not to expect a tiara and a glittery gown, but won't she look somehow different? Special? Royal? I wonder.

When she appears in her doorway, wearing black pants and a very non-descript, hip-length leather jacket, I'm a bit disappointed. This princess would easily blend into a crowd.

Seated next to this fifty-something princess at the ballet, I keep telling myself, "I'm sitting next to a real princess!" During the intermission, the princess and I chat a bit. She speaks English well and listens patiently as I attempt to converse in Italian.

Katharina, who is sitting in another row, comes to talk with us and asks me how I'm enjoying the ballet. I feign interest but she sees through me. She rolls her eyes and taps her watch to let me know her true feelings. Katharina and I share a laugh when Gabrielle joins us and effuses about how much fun she is having.

When Gabrielle and I end up in the ladies room together, she tells me the princess has had some recent health problems and is recovering. The more I'm privy to the lives of the rich and, if not famous at least, prominent, I'm reminded that money and prestige can open doors and make a million things easier, but, as clichéd as it sounds, they cannot guarantee happiness or health.

Gabrielle has told me many times that she is "very busy because I have many things to do." I always find this funny in a Yogi Berra kind of way. But what's not so funny is that in reality Gabrielle is bound by obligation and bored by most of it. Katharina, while impeccably dressed and charming, seems lonely much of the time. And the princess is a flesh and blood person who has to play the cards dealt to her just like everyone else.

Very little is needed to make a happy life; it is all within yourself, in your way of thinking.

–Marcus Aurelius

Volunteering

Gabrielle is chairing a fundraising gala for a non-profit. She invites John and me, but John is swamped with his work at university and the tickets are not in our budget so I beg off and ask to help out in another way. Gabrielle immediately assigns me to help the caterer prepare food for the evening. I love that! I'll get to help the cause, see the *crème de la crème* of Rome at a fancy gala, and, since I'll be wearing an apron, won't have to stress about what to wear. It's perfect.

Taking the bus from Trastevere to Piazza Barbarini, I walk several blocks to the gala venue, the Villa Medici. Located above the Spanish Steps, the facade is dark and imposing and more than a little intimidating. It was built in the sixteenth century and is named for Cardinal Ferdinando de' Medici who purchased it in 1576. Since 1803, it has been the home of the

French Academy, where French painters and musicians have studied while living in Rome.

Because I'm not used to riding the buses yet and am not sure exactly where I'm going, I have allowed extra time in case I miss the stop or get lost en route. The last thing I want is to disappoint Gabrielle, who has shown me such hospitality since arriving in Rome. Getting lost and showing up late is not an option.

Finding the Villa Medici isn't difficult after all, and I'm at least an hour early. The arched doors are gigantic, at least thirty feet tall and, not surprisingly, locked. No one answers when I press the door's buzzer. Out of nowhere, a man carrying a white shirt in a dry- cleaning bag thrown over his shoulder walks swiftly past me and punches buttons on the intercom. A tiny door, maybe four feet tall, within the massive door creaks open. The mystery man, probably part of the wait staff, ducks his head and enters. I follow, ducking as he has, to clear the doorway.

Aside from this man, who quickly disappears down a hallway, no one is in sight. To my right is an old marble stairway winding up a stone-covered wall. Curious as to where it leads, I creep up the steps and imagine that if I just leaned on the wall in the right place a secret passageway might open up. It seems like I should be carrying a flashlight because I feel like I'm reenacting the cover of *The Hidden Staircase,* a Nancy Drew book I read growing up.

No one is stopping me as I reach the top of the stairs so I become braver. On the left is a large bathroom with two marble sinks and counter top. There is a simple bouquet of fresh flowers adding life to this windowless room. It is cool and spacious, but at the same time uncluttered and inviting. I begin to lose perspective and decide if I should ever build a home, I want a bathroom just like this one. It takes several minutes for me to come back to Earth and remember this would be prohibitively expensive.

I wander around a bit more and eventually find someone who directs me to the kitchen at the other end of the villa. The caterer, a French ex-pat and friend of Gabrielle, hands me a white apron and puts me to work making the *crostini,* small toasted slices of French bread topped with *Pâté de Foie Gras* a.k.a. goose liver spread or Camembert cheese. Spreading the *pâté* over the little rounds of bread, I'm finding bits of bumpy skin, a tiny piece from what looks like a webbed foot, and some disgusting, aorta-looking tubes. Ugh! I cannot imagine eating this.

With a little extra care, I'm able to smooth the *pâté* around a bit to disguise the questionable parts. When I have finished making several plates of these appetizers, the caterer advises me to remove anything that looks like "skin or intestine." Oops! The servers have already whisked away the ones I've finished and delivered the appetizers to the guests. I guess they are a hit, because the plates come back empty and I don't hear of any complaints.

The gala features a famous French vocalist, someone unfamiliar to me but obviously popular with this audience of wealthy Europeans. During intermission, Katharina stops by to say hello. She sweeps in wearing a floor-length ball gown and carrying a tiny beaded handbag. She looks adorable, but as usual she also looks a bit bored with her social life. She asks me for some of the *hors d'oeuvres* I prepared earlier and looks disappointed when I tell her there is nothing left to eat. I suggest she check the bar since they might have some pretzels or nuts. Katharina opens her evening bag to show me its contents—empty save for a single tube of lipstick. I offer her some lire, but she is unwilling to take it.

Still during the intermission, Gabrielle, who has been schmoozing as many dignitaries as possible, pulls me from the kitchen to the terrace where her friends have gathered. She introduces me as always as *"la mia amica americana,"* which I am happy to be. The fall night air is perfect for stargazing from the meticulously manicured gardens stretching out behind the Villa. This venue in all its beauty has been the draw for many of the gala attendees, who have now congregated on the terrace. People mill around the pair of lion statues and along the pebbled walkways to socialize and have a smoke. Gabrielle moves on to chat with others while several of her friends hang back and ask me about my life. Why do I live in Rome? What do I do?

"Mio marito è uno studente," my husband is a student, I say and am met with peals of laughter. They're not laughing because I am saying my husband is a student and not a teacher. They are laughing at me.

"Mio marrrrrrito," cackles one of the women, making fun of my pronunciation. Apparently I'm not rolling my rrrr's well enough. These elegantly dressed women decide to teach me this most important lesson on the spot. As they encircle me, their faces just inches from mine, they roll their rrrr's so I can hear what I'm supposed to sound like.

"Mio marrrrrrrrito, marrrrrrrrito, mio marrrrrrrrito." I try to imitate them, but they shake their heads. Coming even closer and opening their mouths wide, they point to the roofs of their

mouths to show me how the tongue must rub up against the roof for correct pronunciation. I'm privy to dental work only a professional should see as they continue to chant in increasing loudness, *"Mio marrrrrrito, MARRRRRRRITO! MIO MARRRRRRRRRRITO!"*

My face is as hot as fire as other guests pause their conversations and look our way. My newfound language teachers are not put off one bit and continue their instruction for what seems like an eternity. I do my best and they seem satisfied with my progress when chimes indicate the end of intermission. *Grazie a Dio!*

I'm relieved to escape to the kitchen and begin helping the caterer tidy up and pack up his white delivery van. When we finish and are ready to depart, the caterer proudly presents me with a small wheel of Camembert cheese and my very own jar of *Pâté de Foie Gras* — intestines and all—to take home. Oh, boy, goodie, goodie.

Tucking them under my arm and exiting the *Villa Medici,* I'm happy to have had a part in this evening's fundraiser, but equally happy to be going home to our little *appartamento* in Trastevere. Maybe one of our neighbors will enjoy the *pâté and* cheese. As for me, toast with butter and blackberry jam makes the perfect late night snack.

Supposing is good, but finding out is better.

−Mark Twain

First in Line

I met Gabrielle a few times at the foundation's office near Campo de' Fiori. One time Gabrielle needed to run some errands, and she invited me to come along. We walked to the French caterer's shop near the French Embassy. She bought a few bottles of wine and some other French comestibles, "for the house." When we popped into the very popular bakery, Antico Forno Rosciolo, the crowd was thick. I imagined it would take quite a while for us to make our way up to the front to place our order with one of the two or three bakers behind the counter. Gabrielle has thought otherwise.

Unapologetically, she moves to the far left side of the crowd and marches to the front of the line in a matter of seconds and places her order for spinach calzone. A minute later we are on our way while the other patrons still stand there, jostling in the pack.

A few days later, I am craving a spinach calzone and decide

to test Gabrielle's strategy. Did the bakers personally know Gabrielle or did her air of self-entitlement produce the desired result? Squeezing in the doorway, I note the place is just as busy as the day Gabrielle and I visited. My head held high, I move quickly to the left and manage to maneuver to the counter. The same baker acknowledges me and takes my order. No waiting. Now these aren't a bunch of tourists in this bakery. Italians make up the majority of the crowd. No one is upset that I was waited on first—at least not that I can tell. I pay and am on my way with my fragrant snack in just a few minutes. Lesson #2 of life as an aristocrat: Act entitled.

I haven't seen Gabrielle for a few weeks when she calls in December to invite me to a luncheon at the home of one of her oldest friends.

I don't realize until we get there that the little bit of Italian I've learned isn't going to do me much good because most of the twenty or so women here are French – part of a large club Gabrielle belongs to. The hostess is a terrific cook and is very proud that she's made most everything herself. The food is to die for: salmon, hummus, couscous and other Greek specialties. After balancing my plate on my lap at this casual luncheon, we gather in the dining room for Champagne toasts and desserts.

Throughout the afternoon, I don't have much to say in French so I amuse myself by counting the number of paintings in the living room (fourteen), making several trips to the two bathrooms on the main floor (one was so large I had to scan the room to find the commode) and filing to memory decorating ideas. It is the most fun locale I've been to with

Gabrielle because the house is full of personality. The walls are yellow with white trim and the sun shines through the many windows, making it undeniably cheery. The hostess has collected art over the years; she and her husband would buy pieces they liked and figure out later where to put them. So it's no surprise their home reflects all kinds of different styles. I can turn one way to find several Egyptian stone figures in one corner of the house and then take ten steps down a corridor to find a French watercolor. Despite the varied pieces, the decor works together beautifully, producing an impressive, albeit eclectic showcase.

During one of my many periods of not having a darn thing to say, I notice a photo on a bookshelf. Isabella, the hostess, sees my startled reaction because she says to me, "Yes, that is the Queen." Staring back at me from the photo are the smiling faces of Isabella, her husband and Queen Elizabeth II, crown and all!

Later in the afternoon, we gather around Isabella while she opens the gifts each guest has brought her. As she unwraps the packages, I'm curious to see what type of expensive and tasteful gifts this affluent crowd has brought. With each gift, I am more disappointed: a small sewing kit, a tchotchke bell, and other unimpressive items. Trinkets. It occurs to me that these gifts could have been bought for anyone. No one has offered an explanation with special meaning or a fun story about why the giver chose this particular item. Could it be that these socially prominent, obviously well-to-do women are re-gifting? The hostess is gracious and seems appreciative, but I have to wonder at what event these items will appear next.

At the end of an afternoon of drinking champagne and eating gourmet desserts, Gabrielle asks if it is okay to drop me off on this side of the Tiber. She zips across town depositing me as promised. She's in a bit of a hurry, but before she drives away she hops out of the car and retrieves a shopping bag from the trunk.

"Buon Natale!" Merry Christmas, she says gaily as she hands me the bag, throws air kisses and jumps back in her car and pulls away. This all happens so fast my head is spinning. Or was it all that champagne?

I'm so turned around that I begin walking the wrong way along the Tiber and get lost. When I finally wend my way home, I open the bag and examine the box wrapped in heavy gold, red and green striped paper and adorned with elaborate gold ribbon. I can't wait until Christmas and open it immediately. Inside the box, a black blouse slinks out of the white tissue paper. I recognize the brand as coming from a store near Via Condotti, one that Gabrielle has mentioned before. I am so touched that she thought of buying me a present and that she spent so much.

Wasting no time, I try on the blouse. It is delicately sheer with an elongated cowl neck, long sleeves and an open back. Sexy, yet sophisticated. I'm not sure I'm up to the task, but I love the idea of wearing it and know I will have to muster the courage somehow. And it wouldn't be long before I have my chance.

I didn't speak Italian when I got to Italy. I had taken a couple of lessons and did a year in college, but in six months, I became regionally submersed to the point that I can curse in dialect.

–Mario Batali

Finding My Inner Italian

At the end of John's first semester, we decide to take a Christmas trip to Naples in the south. We have traveled almost nowhere since our arrival in Rome and feel this break from school is the perfect time to get away. Also, we are worried about feeling homesick over the holidays since none of our family or friends are coming to visit because of the 9/11 attacks.

We take the train from Rome to Naples and, being the frugal Millers, buy bus tickets at the Naples train station instead of hailing a cab to our hotel. The bus is completely full, but we press on with our luggage and are immediately "helped" by old men with caffeinated breath and yellowed or missing teeth. They take our bags, smiling all the while and John and I get separated. We are being worked over and we know it, but we can't move because the bus is so crowded. I can neither see my purse nor move my arm to pull it up closer to my chest. I cling desperately to the strap and hope nothing is being removed. A young Italian woman tells us in English, "You are not safe; you need to get off this bus now." She is sooooo right.

At the next stop, we grab our bags and shove our way off the bus. Standing on the sidewalk, we take inventory. My purse is unzipped, John's jacket's inside pocket containing his passport and wallet is unzipped. On the way to Naples I had read a travel book that mentioned pickpockets so I had moved my cash to the front pocket of my jeans before disembarking from the train. Fortunately, nothing has been taken from either of us, but we are completely freaked out and so grateful for the kind woman's urging.

We pull ourselves together and make our way to the hotel on foot. The reservation we made at the train station showed a picturesque seaside hotel. Hardly. The seaside is picturesque, but the hotel is scary. The elevator to reach the hotel requires lire just to use it, and the surrounding area looks like a bomb strike zone. This is a section of Naples that you never see in the brochures. We search for another hotel and spend more than we want for the security it provides.

Leave it to me and my travel planning; this is the coldest it has been in Naples in fifteen years! We hang out in our hotel room, trying to warm up and calm ourselves from our bus fiasco, but eventually have to get out to take a look around. We are so used to walking and exploring that we have to give Naples a second chance.

We stop in some interesting house-wares shops, one of which sells Alessi. I love Alessi designs for their modern, contemporary and often humorous takes on what are usually ordinary and mundane kitchen and household items. The stainless steel teakettle with the red bird whistle is one of my favorites, but it runs about $175. That acquisition will have to wait for another day.

In a bookshop, I buy a volume from the *Shopaholic* series (go figure) and a deck of cards, in case we hole up in our room playing gin rummy to avoid the frigid temps. We are shivering and not enjoying ourselves too much on this outing when we stop in a bar for hot cocoa. We order two *cioccolate calde,* hot chocolates, and a pastry to share, and I stroll down to the end of the bar looking around. When I hear the barista tell John the bill is 12 euros, I don't think, I just shout, *"Dodici! Che dodici!"* Twelve euros! What twelve euros!

I have barked my outrage in Italian and am promptly rewarded with an apology and a more reasonable tab. My husband gapes at me as if he has never seen me before, and I wonder how I have tapped this inner Italian who speaks the language with such gusto.

I'd like to report that from that moment on my Italian skills are impeccable, that the incident is a breakthrough; that I am able to adopt Italian as a second language, and that I easily converse with any Italian that I meet. Doesn't happen. It is a one off. A fluke. A fight-or-flight reaction.

I continue to struggle with the language, but something does change in me. This out-of-body experience, this alter-ego Martha that has shown up, helps me gain just a slight bit of confidence. Somehow, someway, some of the things that my instructors have been trying to teach me have seeped into my thick skull. It gives me hope.

* * *

Food is always a comfort, and each region of Italy has its specialties. Later than night, John and I begin to finally relax as we discover a local restaurant with world famous Naples pizza. Our Roman neighbor, Loredona, who is originally from Naples, has already introduced me to true Neopolitan pizza. One weekday back in Trastevere she served me lunch, her homemade pizza and *zuppa* (soup), with her and her children. The soup was good, but the pizza was the best I have ever tasted. There is no way to describe the freshness of the tomato sauce or how it melded perfectly with the crust. It is the same here.

The next day we take a taxi to the train station and depart for Sicily. We had initially planned to visit Pompeii, but we've decided to save that for warmer days. The whole idea is to find warmth. We take the train south. At San Giovanni the train breaks apart and boards the ferry. I don't think I would have believed this possible if I hadn't been there to see it with my own eyes. We leave the train car and go up top to see the beautiful view as we cross over to Sicily. Arriving on the Sicilian coast at Messina, we take a bus to Taormina. I have read a lot about Taormina preparing for this trip and it is even better than I imagined. Situated high on a mountain with views of the sea, there are many expensive shops to explore, but the town is also quaint and charming—not intimidating. We have dinner at Nino's Ristorante. The owner, Nino, asks us where we live and what we are doing in Rome. We become so comfortable with him that when he asks if he can order for us and promises that we will love everything, we do not hesitate. We do love everything, including the peach wine he decants by pouring into a colorful, ceramic pitcher. Nino explains that any wine improves if allowed to aerate.

Our *pensione* is cheap, $40 per night, but the heat isn't working too well. We're cold again. The next morning we find out the staff turns the heat off at night to conserve energy! No wonder it was so cold. John doesn't want the hassle of moving to another hotel, but I insist. I find an incredible hotel for the off-season price of $80 per night with fantastic views since it is perched on the side of a mountain, beautifully decorated rooms and a nice breakfast included in the cost.

We visit, the Greek Amphitheatre that is a popular tourist destination because of the setting with spectacular views of the sea and Mount Etna between the columns. At a ceramics store, we buy two pitchers now that Nino has taught us the importance of decanting vino. It gives me a great excuse to buy some souvenirs because we hardly buy anything that we can't eat or use up, as we don't have much room or money to be accumulating things.

We walk down to the beach and have lunch—swordfish, an island specialty, and a tasty pepper, potato, marinated eggplant mixture. We walk back up the mountain, as the funicular is broken and look for the Capuccine monastery. We ask several locals for directions and each one suggests a different path. We walk and walk and walk but cannot locate the monastery. At one point we're climbing higher and higher on a steep path and come upon a home with several chickens wandering loose. It occurs to me that these lucky fowl enjoy a bird's eye view of mountains and sea that most of us would kill for.

Finally I decide the hotel map is useless and leave John to

figure it out while I head back to town to order up a cappuccino and rest my feet.

The next day we catch the intercity train to Messina to head back home. Because of the holidays, it seems all of Italy's population is traveling and we end up standing in the train's corridor for more than three hours. It takes all day to get back to Rome (Sweet Rome). We are tired and hungry and so glad to get back to our little *appartamento*. But when we arrive home, we find no lights, no electricity and no heat!

Apparently our landlord has shut off the power, thinking we have left the country for the holidays. The situation is easily resolved when John runs down to the bottom floor to switch the circuit breaker back on. We've become so used to this practice. It's not only using my hair dryer and the washing machine simultaneously that kick off the power. Turning on the heater, which we have dubbed R2D2, (short, mobile, robot-looking), has often caused a power outage whenever one of these other appliances is running at the same time.

You may have the universe if I may have Italy.

−Giuseppe Verdi

Bringing in the New Year and the Euro

We invite Terri, our upstairs neighbor, to join us for Christmas Eve dinner. She arrives with a bottle of Prosecco, a sparkling Italian wine, to toast the holiday. Terri is leaving the next day. She had originally planned to stay in Rome the entire Christmas break, but her mother sensed her homesickness and sent her a plane ticket to California at the last minute. Before Terri leaves, she offers us the key to the roof of our apartment building. Her apartment on the fifth floor has a skylight, so that she has the right to access a portion of the rooftop that "belongs" with her apartment. We decide to take Terri up on her offer and celebrate New Year's Eve up on the roof.

We planned to go up right before midnight—because, again, it is freezing cold—but about 11:30 p.m. we decide to check out Piazza Santa Maria in Trastevere, which is always full of people at this time. There isn't a soul there! Most of the restaurants are closed and the piazza is dark. Strange. We come back home, grab our bottle of Asti Spumanti (Italian tradition dictates this), two wine glasses and the radio, and head upstairs to the top floor.

To access the roof we unlock a door down the hall from Terri's apartment and climb wooden steps to the exterior door. Once outside, we have a 360-degree view of Rome! Fireworks start a few minutes before midnight, and the radio counts down the last minute of 2001 and then the fireworks really begin in every direction. Everywhere we look the shooting sparks are more amazing than the last. Freezing again, and perched like the pigeons we evicted a few months ago, we toast the New Year, clinking our glasses and sipping the bubbly Prosecco. We love every freezing minute of it, but after two glasses each we can stand the cold no more—time to retreat indoors and start the new year in warmth.

The year 2002 brings the euro (€), which stresses Italians to no end. The conversion to euros is a game-changer for Italians at every socio-economic level. It is a huge adjustment for Italians as lire has been the standard currency since 1861. Not only are there major concerns about the economic ramifications of the changeover primarily inflation, but there are new shapes for bills and eight new coins. Wallet manufacturers are designing all sorts of new styles to hold the new currency.

John and I have just grown accustomed to calculating costs in lire. The euro is based on 100, like U.S. currency, so we aren't thrilled about the change. It makes it too easy, too much like what we are used to at home. But the money is pretty. The crisp colored bills look similar to Monopoly money in pink, blue, green, and yellow, but they aren't as much fun as the game or as lire.

With lire, I loved knowing I had £50,000 in my pocket. It made me feel rich even if it was only about $25. And just as the same grocery cashier at Standa had looked upon us with pity at our confusion with lire during our first grocery-shopping excursion, we now empathize with her as she tries to make change for us in euros.

I find television very educating. Every time somebody turns on the set, I go into the other room and read a book.

—Groucho Marx

Italian Television

John and I have been living in Italy for a few months when we decide to buy a television. It is so quiet in the apartment we justify that having a TV (or as Italians pronounce it *"tee voo"*) would allow us to watch the news, improve our language skills, and all the while tune in, pun intended, to Italian culture in a different way.

Italian television is different to say the least. The used set we purchase opens our eyes when one of the first commercials we view literally exposes a topless woman in a bubble bath. *Mamma mia!*

Evening game shows and even morning talk shows feature *veline,* which are a bevy of beautiful young women dressed in identical sexy outfits. The purpose of these teams of young dancers, mostly twenty-something, is to serve unapologetically as eye candy. Unlike Vanna White or the models on *The Price is Right*, these women do not display items or point to prizes, though one may hold a sign occasionally or banter with the host. Their sole purpose is to exude sexiness, wearing ever-more provocative costumes. It is startling to me to see a scantily clad woman - think Vegas showgirl - standing on the television host's desk at 9:00 a.m. as he, dressed in a well- made Italian suit, begins his show. During the program, he may ascend the aisle to talk to guests. Several of the girls will be standing strategically on the aisle steps behind him; smiling all the while he is conversing with a guest. The most popular members of these groups become celebrities in their own right, appearing in tabloid magazines and becoming romantically linked to famous actors, musicians or soccer players.

I particularly love watching the evening newscasts of one female anchor. This woman is fifty-something, and every bit the *bella figura*. She sports sparkly or silky blouses showing ample cleavage. Her plumped-up lips, immaculately groomed hair and makeup are perfect. There is no downplaying her femininity in dark suits or boring button downs. She is beautiful and smart. Her intelligence and confidence show through with her no-nonsense delivery of the news.

It's also great fun to watch American television shows dubbed in Italian. The daytime soap opera, " *The Bold and the Beautiful,*" which is known in Italy simply as *"Beautiful,"* is one of the most popular shows in the country. One day, I hear the sounds of Signora Oberti's television drift through our open windows. I immediately realize she is watching *"Beautiful"* because I am too. When I see her a few days later, I bring up the topic of the show and she and I have one of our best conversations ever. We discuss, in Italian, the love triangle between Brooke/*madre,* her daughter/*figlia* Bridget and Bridget's boyfriend/*fidanzato* Deacon. We laugh and laugh as we are able to finally communicate about something besides the weather – our favorite characters and their *comportamento male* or bad behavior. Juicy gossip—a cultural connection!

Truly, the commercials have to be the best part of Italian television. One of my favorites is about a vacuum cleaner. A hip-looking mom is pushing the vacuum all around the house. Before long, she hears a clink under the machine and discovers her belly button jewel. She pops it in and goes merrily on her way. Infinitely more interesting than watching dog hair getting sucked up.

And then there is the *Buonnnnaaaaa serrrrrrrra* commercial. A beautiful woman is going ballistic on the telephone. The actress is speaking so fast, we have no idea what she is saying, except that it is obvious she's furious. Luigi, one of our neighbors and Loredona's husband, explains it to us.

The woman is screaming into the receiver that she is going to go with the next man she meets. A neighbor, overhearing her rant, plants himself outside her door so that when she steps out, he's leaning against the doorway and suavely introduces himself saying, *"Buonnnnaaaaa serrrrrrra."*

The spot didn't blatantly focus in on a product, so we never even realized what they were selling. The message we got was much more about grabbing attention and, boy, did it!

I was standing in a crowded *salumeria* a few weeks after this commercial started airing and one of the patrons in the back loudly greets his friend behind the counter with,

"Buonnnnnnaaaaa serrrrrrra." The whole crowd, including me, erupts in laughter; in that instant, I feel a cultural connection with these Italians. I would have never known what was so funny without our *tee voo* and Luigi.

We decide it also makes sense to get Internet at the apartment. My feeble attempt to get it connected over the telephone doesn't go well. It's even harder to communicate in a language you're not fluent in over the phone. When I can't understand her questions, I ask the account representative if I can email her and she gives me her email address. The next day, I ask Rosalba, a friend I have met who works at the university, for help. She writes a fantastic letter for me that we email to the cable company that day. A couple of weeks later while John and I are dining *al fresco* at Osteria der Belli, one of our favorite restaurants in the neighborhood, my phone starts ringing in my purse next to the table. It is after 8:00 p.m. so I'm surprised to find the customer service department is calling so late. I answer the phone but still can't answer her questions. Somehow I manage to relate that I will call back the next day, and cut the call short.

At the university the next day, I ask Rosalba to call the rep for me. She does and is able to get our account set up and in the queue for a service call to connect the modem.

The customer service representative tells Rosalba, "For her (me) to write in Italian so well, I don't understand why she can't speak Italian better."

No need to hurry; the connection will take at least a month, Rosalba is told. It actually ends up taking three months, four days and many more phone calls.

*To be yourself in a world that is constantly trying to make you
something else is the greatest accomplishment.*
                                    –Ralph Waldo Emerson

Cristina's Dinner Party

I first met Cristina, a new Italian friend, at the train station in
Trastevere. I was planning to take the train to the airport to
meet my mother who was finally coming for a visit several
months after the 9/11 attacks. Cristina was on her way to meet
someone as well. We waited and waited and waited for the
train and finally discovered that it wasn't running because of a
strike. In Italy, strikes are common, short lived and generally
thought to accomplish nothing. This one lasted for a couple of
hours in the middle of the day.

Cristina and I had begun chatting during our wait and
with the news of the strike decided to share a cab to the
airport. She had been an exchange student in the United States
during high school and spoke English perfectly. She was kind
to let me practice my Italian with her and, as we parted ways at
the airport, she suggested we get together again.

I called her a few weeks later after my mother had left and

we met for *caffè*. Soon after, she invited John and me to a dinner party at her apartment in Campo de' Fiori. We are thrilled to be included with her Italian friends, and I am sure that wearing the sheer, black blouse Gabrielle gave me for Christmas will make me look every bit the *fashionista* I aspire to be.

Still clinging to American customs, we arrive at Cristina's on time. The buzzer goes unanswered so we mill around outside for a while. Punctuality is pointless in Rome because no one expects it but it's a hard habit for us to break. I take the opportunity to adjust my top and check my lipstick one more time. Finally, Cristina passes by a window, sees us and calls out to come on up—apparently the buzzer is broken.

When the other guests arrive at least an hour later, a new mom is dressed very cute but not sexy at all. Her knit jumper and white tee is something I would normally wear, and I wish I had. Other women and men are wearing sweaters and snug jeans or pants – it's February after all and Italians dislike intently being cold.

My back is exposed and the sheer fabric of my blouse feels thinner by the minute. I perch on the black leather sofa, carefully pressing my back firmly against the cushions and hoping I blend in. When Cristina calls us to dinner, I delay as long as possible, not wanting the men waiting for me to see my bare back when I exit the room.

At dinner, I want to tuck my napkin into the large cowl neck to hide my black brassiere showing through the sheer fabric. This is one of those naked nightmares come to life. Italian dinner lasts for hours, and I yearn to fetch my coat but do not lest I draw more attention to my embarrassment. For the rest of the evening, I don't remember the conversations around the dinner table or what was served, only that I feel or imagine too many eyes on my chest and too much air on my back.

A week or two later, while sipping *cappuccini* outdoors at a café near Piazza Trilussa, Cristina and I discuss the different ways Americans and Italians dress.

We observe an American exchange student sitting by herself at a table wearing a short wrap skirt, tank top and no bra. It's too chilly for this outfit, and I'm uncomfortable watching as her body reacts to the cold. It reminds me of my fashion fiasco at Cristina's dinner party. While I try to shove the image of my bare back out of my mind, Cristina says, "Italians would assume that girl is easy."

I counter, saying, "I think Americans would think she lacks common sense." I look at the American exchange student as I'm saying this, but really, I'm thinking of myself.

Cristina agrees there doesn't seem to be a bridge between the young trendy and the older matronly style. Ah, except for Gabrielle, who, after all, is really French and knows how to dress well at any age, and perhaps one woman – an Italian - I see regularly coming and going that lives one floor below us.

My apartment building actually houses a microcosm of Italian dressers. On the top floor, Zia Maria, Signora Oberti's aunt by marriage, and her husband Aldo, have lived in the building for sixty years. I am taller than both of them, being just over five feet in stature. Maria always wears one of her print dresses topped with a neatly buttoned cardigan sweater. Whenever they return from grocery shopping, Aldo drops Maria and the grocery bags off in front of our building while he parks their tiny aqua-colored car. She climbs the four flights of stairs slowly in flat shoes and off-white socks. Whenever I see her, I just want to do things for her. She is not frail, but she looks tired. Her white hair frames her kind face and she is always so appreciative when John and I insist on carrying the bags the rest of the way for her. "*Sei molto gentile.*" You're very kind, she would say. "*Niente,*" we respond. We wish we could do more.

Terri, the other American ex-pat in the building lives on the same floor as Maria and Aldo. Keeping true to her Californian roots, she never hesitates to adopt a fashion trend, even if it is impractical. One day, I stare in amazement as she ascends the stairs wearing jeans that drag at least an inch and a half past the heel of her boots. I can't help but think of them sweeping over the filthy streets and how they must harbor *caca* from the neighborhood canines.

Loredana, who is Luigi's wife and the one who taught me about true Naples pizza, is the closest we have to a *fashionista*. This mother of two small children, Claudia, four, and Davide, two, was a fashion designer before becoming a stay-at-home mom. She wears slim-fitting jeans and trendy sweaters and blouses always accessorized with sunglasses and funky handbags.

I've dubbed one of my neighbors Ms. Sophisticate. She lives alone on the floor below us and is probably in her early sixties. Whenever I see her in passing, her thick auburn hair is meticulously blown out in a sleek bob. She dresses in tailored slacks and rich-colored sweaters accessorized with scarves and jeweled pins. Her finishing touch is, without fail, donned dark sunglasses, even in the hallway.

Several times I try to make conversation with her, but she is brusque, always in a rush and disinterested in politeness or us. She radiates superiority along with a good bit of snobbishness. This air of mystery is fascinating and makes me want to get to know her all the more. I imagine that she works in publishing or art collecting. Sometimes when I see her emerging from her apartment, I catch a glimpse of the inside to see scarlet walls, muted lighting, and bookshelves that extend the length of the substantial entryway and lined with stacks of books and highbrow *objets*. On a good day, Ms. Sophisticate nods at us. More often than not she merely grunts in our direction or simply fails to muster any type of greeting as she swiftly turns her key and shuts the door.

I do what I can to look the part of bona fide Romans, despite our shoe- string budget. Wearing black and denim seems to be cool enough, though my jeans aren't as holey, nor are they adorned with feathers or fur, or drag across the ground like they should. But I do okay. It's easier during winter when I can throw my black leather jacket on and wrap a colorful scarf around my neck.

The clothing store down the *vicolo* always has such attractive window displays that salivate every time I pass by. The bespectacled owner regularly stands outside and greets passersby, which makes it harder to just walk on by.

One day, I am strolling by during *riposo* when that favorite store is closed. An outfit in the display window is so fabulous that it catches my eye. I take in the black, wool trousers, the cut of its wide leg, and study the salt and pepper nubby-yarn sweater. I squeeze myself between the display window and the micro-car parked in front and imagine how fabulous I would look in this Italian outfit when: SLURCH! My eye for fashion has landed me in a pile of dog poop! *CACA!*

Undeterred, I return for a second look when the store is open and the stop becomes the Campo de' Fiori shopping trip redux. The owner and a saleswoman tell me that everything I try on looks, *"Bella, molto bella!* I've been going through fashion withdrawal and rationalize that I haven't bought anything in months—it's time for a splurge. I exit the store 45 minutes later with a bag full of new clothes: the fabulous black trousers from the window display; a black calf-length, gabardine skirt; and a sweater with leather insets and a zillion tiny silver hooks and eyes to clasp in the front. Sexy, but still warm. With this new outfit, I need coordinating shoes and know just where to find them. Next stop is Jacques Calzature, where I previously spotted the perfect pair of boots—black leather, with two buckled straps wrapping around the ankle, very pointy, and three-inch heels! €25. Done! I lack a specific purpose for this outfit, but am convinced it will come in handy. And it does.

Whatever you want to do, do it now. There are only so many tomorrows.

−Michael Landon

Running in Rome's Race for the Cure®

Rome, Italy hosted the first Komen Race for the Cure® ever held in Europe in 2000. Having run the Komen 5k in Houston a few times before, I have been looking forward to participating in the Rome race since I arrived. I signed up for the 2002 race with a group from the university. The plan was to meet at the entrance before the start of the race to retrieve the official t- shirt and number bib. John would come along to take pictures.

What's that proverbial saying about the best laid plans? The night before the race, John comes down with a bad case of food poisoning and the next morning isn't able to leave the bathroom, much less the apartment. At the race site, faced with the hordes of people, I can't find anyone from the university at our designated meeting place.

Hoping to run into someone I know, I walk around Race Village (Terme di Caracalla), where vendors have set up booths. On one end, an assembly from Jazzercise is conducting a dance routine to warm up. They do that in the U.S. too, and it is reassuring to see the familiar banner and dance moves. At the opposite end of the field, a children's play area features an inflated bounce house replicating the Colosseum, complete with tiger and gladiator figures. I'm not sure if Houston's Race has a play area for kids, but if they do it might include a NASA theme with spaceship and astronauts. What a contrast that would be!

I make my way to where I think the race is going to start. I wait. And wait. At least fifteen minutes past the start time, people are still milling around. I shouldn't expect punctuality in Italy, but I do expect to hear gun fire, the release of white doves or some kind of signal that the race is starting. I am frustrated, out of sync and homesick for my Houston girlfriends, Cynthia and Suzy, with whom I always ran the Race for the Cure, when suddenly people start running past me. Apparently I am not as near to the start line as I thought. Without thinking, I jump over the rope barrier and join the runners, hoping that no one will pull me out because I am not wearing an official race number.

We run along Circus Maximus, a long, grassy field where chariot races, not charity events, once took place. Italian names line the backs of the other runners, honoring the women in their lives who have won, are fighting or have lost their battle with breast cancer. My heart aches for their mothers, grandmothers, sisters, wives, aunts, cousins and friends.

We make our way to Piazza Venezia. On any other day, this popular thoroughfare would be jammed with frenetic drivers, honking horns, buses filled to capacity and groups of tourists with cameras swaying from their necks, but this day is different. With no *traffico*, the melodic sounds of laughter and beautifully spoken Italian rise above the pounding of thousands of feet against the pavement.

When we tackle an incline and circle the Colosseum, I slow down and take in the moment. The morning's cloudless blue sky is a perfect backdrop to stone arches built nearly two thousand years ago. The always- breathtaking Colosseum looms in stark contrast to Houston's post-modern skyline. The setting is surreal, sending a shot of adrenaline through my body, and brings me back to the race.

I sprint toward the finish line, which is apparently of much more importance than the start line, because it is well marked with balloons and banners. Spectators cheer us on as we pass through. By the time I reach the vendor booths, they are teeming with participants eager for swag. Apparently the thrill of scoring free stuff transcends nationalities.

Families gather in the grassy area of Race Village to relax, to listen to bands playing and to watch *bambini* bouncing in the air- filled Coliseum. Though I am alone, I am glad I have made the effort to be here in this moment, participating in the Italian Komen Race for the Cure.

The after-party doesn't include rows of tables lined with bananas, bagels or yogurt like they have in Houston, so on my walk home I treat myself to a *cornetto. Delizioso,* a perfect post-race refuel to my first Old World race.

...and forgive us our trespasses, as we forgive those who trespass against us.

– The Lord's Prayer

Rooftop Lesson

Despite several months of intensive language classes, *la mia amica italiana* Gabrielle insists that I switch language schools. She is displeased with my slow progress, so she places a call and soon I am taking inexpensive classes that meet only one day a week at a local university. After taking the placement test, I am placed in beginning Italian yet again. It is a crushing realization, but at least I figure I'll have a fighting chance.

John and I do a run-through beforehand so I know how to get to my new class. It only involves taking a bus from Trastevere and walking a few blocks. My class meets from 7:00 to 8:30 p.m. The classes are in Prati, an upscale area of Rome with expensive shops and larger, more modern cafés. Candy store displays are absolute works of art. I find a designer clothing outlet and always try to get there before class to look around since it will be closed afterward.

My new teacher, Daniele, is kind, and I like that he doesn't move us along too fast.

Unfortunately, the honeymoon ends too soon. Because Daniele thinks we're having so much fun and doing so well, he starts holding class twice a week. And just like the other classes, my bewilderment starts to snowball, and I can feel myself getting flattened.

I continue to attend class – I want to be there, I just don't want to get called on. I keep hoping something will click and I'll get over this hump. I can't compare it to anything but a complete brain freeze when I'm called on in class. My mind ceases to comprehend anything, and I can't form a response, much less know what I'm being asked. It's awful and I'm terribly disappointed.

I do my homework and practice conversational sentences to use when shopping, which work pretty well. But in the classroom, it's a different story. I try everything to boost my confidence and comprehension. Buy a used television to watch talk shows, news programs, and American shows dubbed in Italian. Read "stupid magazines," as one well-meaning storeowner suggests, in Italian. Attend Italian Mass. Eavesdrop on conversations. I even start chewing gum after reading an article about a study that claimed chewing gum while studying increases students' comprehension.

One night Daniele asks me to stay after class. As I'm gathering up my books and bag, another student comments on Daniele's request. Huh? Thankfully she has mentioned it because I completely missed his request. If there were an award for most pathetic student, I would have nailed it.

At our "conference" Daniele mentions that he has noticed I'm struggling and offers to tutor me during the next few weeks. He says we have a test coming up, and he knows there is no way I'll pass. I agree to meet him twice a week outside of class and the first lesson will be at my place. This first of my private lessons turns out to be a fiasco, but for once the reason does not lie in my lack of language skills.

It is a very warm day for my first lesson. Daniele is already wiping sweat from his brow just from climbing the three flights of stairs to my apartment. My home provides very little relief from the heat. He asks if we can move our studies to the rooftop. I still have Terri's key, which gives me access to the roof. Terri has allowed us to keep it, and encouraged us take advantage of it. We don't need to be told twice.

Ascending to the roof immediately awakens our senses. It is lovely with cool breezes sweeping across the roof. The view of the domed city is spectacular. I am mesmerized and feeling so comfortable that I allow myself to overlook one small, yet critical detail: the rooftop is no longer mine to enjoy. Terri has graduated recently and moved back to California. She never asked us to return the key. I have never seen anyone else up here, and I don't think John and I are hurting anyone by slipping up here occasionally to sip a Tanqueray and tonic while taking in the night air. Besides, looking down through the skylight into Terri's former apartment, I conclude it has remained vacant since Terri's departure. Rationalization at its best.

As Daniele and I settle into flimsy, white plastic chairs on Terri's side, the sun begins beating down on us. Daniele asks if we can move to the other side of the rooftop, where there is an awning shading a table and chairs.

I am uncomfortable with the suggestion and attempt to dissuade him, but he is sweating profusely and practically begging me to agree. I inspect the other side, with its vine-covered archway and fragrant potted hibiscus plants. It is awfully inviting and hard to resist.

Okay, what's the harm? No one's ever come up here when I've been here before so why not? I reason. I relent because John has joined us by now and has voiced no disagreement. The three of us leave behind our flimsy chairs and settle under the awning. We are in the midst of practicing conversational skills when the terrace door swings wide open and a tan, muscular man— Signore Green Thumb of the hibiscus plants, I presume— bounds out, looking mad as hell. Who can blame him? We have laid claim to his carefully tended oasis, sprawled out on his side of the rooftop with a stack of language books and beverages in hand. We might as well have been three strangers playing Twister in his living room.

It might have been the blazing heat or his absolute rage, most likely both, but his face has turned scarlet. His crystal blue eyes are opened wide, his mouth gaping. I have rarely seen this thirty- something neighbor and have never met him, but I certainly recognize him even with the furious look he now wears.

All I can say to him is, *"Mi dispiace,"* "I'm sorry," over and over again. It is a feeble response but my deep embarrassment has frozen the words in my mouth.

All he can say in return is, "But this is *my* side." He is so outraged that he doesn't even yell. He merely repeats the phrase over and over, in perfect English.

John, Daniele and I gather up our books and beverages,

and sheepishly exit the rooftop. Daniele leaves the building; Italian lesson is cut short for the day. John seems to blow off our encounter with our red-faced neighbor after returning home, but I am not so easily appeased. An ill feeling has settled in my gut and I feel like throwing up.

If only that had been the end of it. A few days later John and I are on "our side" of the rooftop trying to enjoy gin and tonics, though I am a little nervous about being up here again. Sure enough, Signore Green Thumb returns. He can't stand that we are up here and peppers us with questions as to how we have a key, to whom does it belong, and why we are up here. We don't stay long enough to answer all his queries.

I begin to run into this neighbor ALL the time. On the stairs, at the front door, along the *vicolo*—he seems to be everywhere. He corners me on the stairwell a few days later and interrogates me again about the key. This time he tells me he spoke with the owner of the skylight apartment and that she confirmed she hasn't given anyone else permission to use the rooftop. He is unrelenting.

John and I decide the best thing to do is to return the key to the university staffer who works with the landlady. That way we won't incur blame for anything else that might happen up there. We sure do miss our rooftop retreat, though I don't think I'll ever order a Tanqueray and tonic without thinking of that rooftop, and unfortunately, Signore Green Thumb.

You can observe a lot by watching.

–Yogi Berra

Mass Chaos

Rome has many churches all within steps of each other. A few weeks after our move to Rome, John and I found the church where we feel most comfortable—Santa Dorotea, which is just a short walk down our *vicolo* from our building. From the outside, the structure is so non- descript that you'd pass right by unless you were looking for it. Wedged between a faded red apartment building and a melon- colored one, the light orange, concave façade is all that is visible from the street.

But inside, our eyes see beauty wherever they rest. The church, which has been rebuilt twice, is now decorated in 18th century Baroque style. It is such a delight to enter into this hidden gem to enjoy frescoes and impressive works from lesser-known artists from Rome, Florence and Vienna. Overlooked by guidebooks and tourists, it feels like our own special discovery.

The priest and his deacon are Franciscan so they wear traditional humble brown robes with a rope tied at the waist, which only adds to the Old World feel of the church. A plaque on the wall—"1991"—proudly marks the year Pope John Paul II visited, a modern reminder in this anachronistic church. What adds even more to the ambiance are the cold drafts swirling around our legs in the fall and winter. In those chilly months, John and I would vie for the seat closest to the space heater placed in the aisle on the frostiest days.

Rome, in its modernity, continually surprises me. With its rich Catholic history, I expect Romans to march to Mass with devotion, to go through these motions with pious dedication. But what John and I discover, instead, is that Masses are usually sparsely populated. People rarely attend Mass and children are hard to find in churches. Because of this, it is easy to pick out the regulars at Santa Dorotea, and because we live a stone's throw from the church, we often spy them going about their daily business in the neighborhood and especially at my favorite open-air *mercato* in Piazza San Cosimato.

The majority of the services are conducted in Italian, but Padre Paul, a priest from a Midwestern Catholic college is assigned to Italian and English Masses. We became well acquainted with Padre Paul and enjoy his company. He introduces us to some great restaurants in Trastevere—a robust man who savors a good meal; Padre Paul knows the best dishes to order at each dining establishment.

One weekend, Padre Paul is well into giving his sermon in Italian when a petite, elderly woman, walking with a cane, enters the church and slowly shuffles down the center aisle. As is typical, the church on this day is more than three-quarters empty. Though there are numerous vacant pews flanking her, she passes them all up, albeit at a snail's pace, and pointedly makes her way to the front of the altar. I doubt anyone else is listening to Padre Paul's sermon as we wait for her to take her seat. But that is precisely the problem. When she reaches the second row, she abruptly stops to find someone in "her seat."

The old woman says something undecipherable to the woman "occupying" her spot, but the interloper refuses to budge. The elderly woman keeps standing and lifts her left hand holding her cane to motion for this other woman to release her seat. Finally, Padre Paul stops his sermon, smiles, and gently says, *"Prego."* He holds out his hand and gestures for the woman to take a seat. Still she refuses. An uncomfortable silence descends for what seems like an eternity until, finally, the seated woman scoots over a *little.* The elderly woman takes "her" seat by squeezing in next to her. Padre Paul can now resume his sermon.

After Mass, we ask Padre Paul if the incident broke his concentration. He responds, "Oh, that was nothing. You should see what I see from the altar. It's a zoo."

Interesting choice of words, Padre, I think. In Europe, it isn't unusual to see dogs in restaurants, hotels, and even churches. In our church, a young English woman, Beth, who works as a tour guide at the Vatican, brings her new puppy, Charlie, to Mass with her nearly every week. Beth is in the process of becoming a Catholic, and she is devout in her prayers before, during and after the Mass. One weekend, John and I are in Mass sitting a few rows behind Beth, with Charlie sitting on the floor near Beth's feet. We watch Charlie diligently chewing on his leash during the homily. Beth is listening intently to the sermon and oblivious to Charlie's activity. Charlie finally manages to chew through the leash; finding himself free, he starts wandering the aisles exploring this new territory. It doesn't take him long to find his way up to the altar. When Beth realizes Charlie has escaped, she starts calling to him in a whisper, but he happily ignores her and continues up the steps to where Padre Paul is preaching. Charlie is enthusiastically sniffing the Padre's feet. Beth, thoroughly mortified, approaches the altar, grabs Charlie by the scruff of the neck and hauls him back to the pew.

Another animal incident at Santa Dorotea involves a large dog "parked" under the holy water font near the back of the church. A latecomer to Mass accidentally steps on the dog's foot, causing him to yelp loudly. A boisterous exchange ensues between the dog's owner, the priest, the latecomer, and the dog who joins in the squabble about whether canines belong in church by "voicing" his own side of the argument. The exchange echoes through the cavernous church, amplifying an exciting, tense and laughable moment. Mass is never dull.

While we attend Santa Dorotea Saturday evenings for Padre Paul's English Mass, our neighbors Maria and Aldo attend the Italian Mass held right before our English Mass. If John and I encounter Aldo and Maria coming up the marble stairs as we race down, we know we are late. If we pass them returning from Mass on the street, we know we still have a couple of minutes to get to Mass on time. They always smile and wave us on not to be tardy. You could set your clock by Maria and Aldo.

Occasionally, we attend another church in our neighborhood because the timing works better for something else we want to do. Santa Maria, located in the eponymous piazza in Trastevere, is our choice one Sunday morning. Unlike Santa Dorotea, this church is very popular with tourists, who often ignore the posted signs pleading that Mass not be interrupted. It is hard to stay focused with the sermon given in Italian, and then doubly so with tourists strolling along the sides of the pews, craning their necks to gaze at the intricate ceiling and gawking and pointing at the rich details.

We are well into the second half of the service when, as is customary, the priest asks the congregation to share the sign of peace with each other. This can mean a handshake, a hug with those you know, maybe a kiss with your honey or a smile and a nod to those who are not within arm's reach. I recognize some of the attendees as locals. The lady in the pew in front of us with a long, white-gray ponytail is a Trastevere resident. I have seen her many times walking her pet ferret on a leash. It has always unnerved me a bit, because at first glance the ferret looks like a small dog, then a rat, and then the realization hits that it is a ferret.

When Ponytail turns to share the sign of peace, tucked into her blouse, snuggled between her breasts, is the ferret. The small rodent is facing out with his little paws held up like a miniature kangaroo. I am so startled I almost scream, but Ponytail's expression doesn't give anything away. She acts as though this is the only way one could possibly carry her ferret to church as if this is a common occurrence.

Yes, Padre Paul, it is a zoo out here.

I always know the ending; that's where I start.

–Toni Morrison

Getting Published

Long before living abroad became my dream, I dreamed of becoming a writer. In fifth grade, I wrote a story about becoming a writer like Louisa May Alcott when I grew up. I think it made an impression on me when the character Jo in *Little Women* was paid for a story. *You mean you can get paid for writing? Sign me up!*

I didn't pursue it seriously though. I enjoyed writing essays in high school and college English and received encouraging comments from my professors, but I pursued a business degree and enjoyed my marketing classes — practical studies that would ensure a steady paycheck.

In Rome, after deciding Italian was no longer my full-time job, the itch to make some money consumed me, and I decided the time was right to give writing a real try. I had given freelance writing a try a few times before, but had never seriously pursued it. This time was going to be different. I lived in Rome, Italy, one of the most, if not the most, beautiful and historic cities in the world. Maybe now I could find something to write about. I wasn't interested in writing about history, architecture, art or religion, not that I was the slightest bit qualified to do so. I knew none of these subjects were my niche.

Taking a page from my retail background, I decide my first stab at writing is to "investigate" what Romans consider bad shopping etiquette in Italy. I recall that not long after moving to Rome, I was reproached at a newsstand for flipping through a magazine. Then there was the incident on Via Nazionale when my mother was visiting. She innocently picked up a sandal as we entered a store and was loudly berated for touching what was technically part of the window display.

Italian shopping etiquette does exist, but even with over fifteen years of retail experience in the United States, I was puzzled about étiquette in certain situations. Thinking my mom and I might not be the only ones confused, I decide to get to the bottom of this mystery.

I compose a query letter to the editor of *Wanted in Rome*, an English-language magazine sold at newsstands all across the city. I ask to write an article about what is acceptable and what is considered rude shopping behavior of foreigners. The editor likes the idea and asks me to write the article on spec, which means she may or may not publish it. If she doesn't use it, I will not get paid. I have no previous writing experience and know writing on spec is standard practice for new writers at some publications. I don't have anything to lose.

Thrilled to have an assignment, a *real* writing assignment, I immediately start working on my questions. I have promised the editor to interview storeowners, managers and salespeople in a variety of retail businesses, asking them what constitutes taboo shopping behavior of foreigners. I first prepare my questions in English and then try to translate them into Italian.

Realizing I need help, I run through my list of friends and acquaintances who might be able to help me. Iris, who manages a *cartoleria*, a card shop, in Piazza Santa Maria in Trastevere, is one person who comes to mind. I barely know her, but she has always been cordial whenever I visit her store. I tear down the stairs and up the street to the shop to ask Iris to help me.

Iris is from Austria but has lived in Rome for years. She speaks Italian and English very well and though she doesn't know me well, she quickly agrees to help. She translates the questions— even in some instances changing the phrasing— and then lets me practice asking her the questions in Italian.

Over the next few days I walk all over Rome interviewing shopkeepers with my perfected questions. My first line is to introduce myself and explain my mission. "*Mi chiamo* Martha Miller." Continuing in Italian but more slowly, "*Sto scrivendo un articolo delle maniere brutte degli stranieri*," or "I am writing an article about the bad manners of foreigners." As my words sink in, the vendor, store manager or salesperson inevitably smiles or laughs and usually respond in English. They often take my typed list of questions right out of my hand and write or dictate their answers to me. It is much easier than I expect, and I know my Italian improves measurably as a result. Lesson #1 in Shopping Etiquette: Speak their language. It certainly helps that I began my interviews that way. Within Trastevere, I find that I must continue the entire interview in Italian, but across the Tiber, most shopkeepers are fluent in English and slip into my native tongue.

Everyone I speak with agrees to the interview. They seem to enjoy talking about their business as much as I do. By the end of the week, I have a notebook full of pages of eye-opening information and certainly more than enough material to write the article. I spend a few days drafting the piece, agonizing over every word and turn of phrase before I finally submit it.

Two weeks later, I receive a response. The editor has accepted my article; I am finally going to be a published writer! And I am going to get paid!

Not so fast. The editor tells me I must get a *Codice Fiscale* so they can pay me. She explains this is basically a tax code card (similar to a Social Security card) and she provides the address of the *Agenzia delle Entrate* or tax office in Trastevere where I can apply for one. I knew it! There had to be a catch. This is going to be just like trying to get a dependent visa at the Houston Consulate's office and is either going to take forever or never happen.

Though the tax office appeared to run like a DMV with a crowd of people and numbers being called, it was a swift process. I was in and out in about 10 minutes! Much to my delight, this was the easiest thing I ever had to do in Italy. Getting my *Codice Fiscale* was *simplice*.

Manners are a sensitive awareness of the feeling of others. If you have that awareness, you have good manners, no matter what fork you use.

–Emily Post

Shopping Etiquette, Italian Style

The following is my first published article verbatim, which appeared in *Wanted in Rome on* 1 May 2002.

Shopping Etiquette, Italian Style
By Martha Miller

Do you like to touch and feel when shopping? Are you tempted to pick up items you have no intention of buying just to take a closer look? Have you been chastised for reaching into a window display as if you've defiled sacred ground? If you answered "yes" to any of these questions you may not realize that you have committed shockingly bad behaviour where Italian shopkeepers are concerned.

Italian shopping etiquette does exist, but even with over 15 years of retail experience in the United States I was puzzled as to how to behave in certain everyday situations. I had a vague idea of what was acceptable but found myself being reprimanded on occasion. Thinking I might not be the only one perplexed, I decided to get to the bottom of this mystery.

I asked 31 storeowners, managers and salespeople in a variety of retail businesses what they felt were bad manners, specifically of foreigners. Included in this survey were moderately-priced as well as Via Condotti-priced boutiques specialising in a wide range of merchandise. As an extra benefit, the research provided valuable information regarding exchange and return policies.

First of all, first impressions do count. Respond to being greeted upon entering the store. This is common courtesy and sets a pleasant tone for your shopping experience. Do not assume the seller speaks your language. As Massimo Dipersio, a *giornalaio* in Trastevere, made clear: "I am Italian. I was born in Italy. Why should I speak their language?" Even if you don't speak Italian well, making an effort goes a long way. Eating and drinking are high on the list of things you should not do for obvious reasons. Trailing close behind is smoking. Lighting up is generally considered forbidden. The exception was where the shopkeeper answered questions between puffs. Chatting on a mobile phone grated on the nerves of several people interviewed, including the *giornalaio,* the *tabaccaio* and the produce vendor. If your phone rings make the conversation brief or, better still, take care of business first, move on and then return the call.

About two-thirds of shops said it was not bad from to ask for a discount. As Gerti Derflinger, who has a cartoleria in Trastevere, says: "It isn't rude to ask and I can say no."

More than anything else, handling the inventory is

considered the "touchiest" subject. Not long after moving to Rome, I was reproached at a newsstand for flipping through a magazine. Then there was the incident on Via Nazionale when my mother was visiting. She innocently picked up a sandal as we entered the store and was loudly berated for touching what was technically part of the window display. Window displays are absolutely not to be touched. Many stores only have very little window space and if it is disrupted they cannot put their best face forward. The merchandise in the window is available in the store. Just ask, or smile and point.

How much touching is too much depends on the type of merchandise. At Pier Caranti, a leather goods store in Piazza di Spagna, the owner Federico Calò explained it this way: "Of course it is okay to pick up and feel the leather, but don't unzip and handle roughly." Salespeople will gladly unzip and empty the handbag so you can take a closer look.

Comments were more forceful at high-priced stores with merchandise made from beautiful textiles. For example, exclusive children's apparel and exquisite linen will quickly become shop-worn and unsellable from too much handling. In grocery stores and produce markets it may be considered offensive to touch fruit and vegetables. Use the plastic gloves provided or allow the vendor to bag your choices.

Every retailer with the exception of the produce vendors said they would exchange merchandise if it was presented in perfect condition, accompanied by the receipt, and within a reasonable timeframe: usually one to two weeks. In the case of a manufacturer's defect an exchange would be granted as well. Surprisingly, refunding cash or crediting a charge card is not allowed. Taxes are paid according to what is rung and once the sale is completed on the cash register it cannot be undone. At the designer boutiques near Via Condotti, it is mostly visitors from the United States who are upset by this. The return policies in the States are very liberal and most stores will credit your charge card if you change your mind, as long as the item has not been worn or damaged. It probably never crosses these customers' minds that this may not be the practice in Italy.

Overall, when asked to give an example of the worst behaviour they had witnessed, most merchants were hard-pressed to relay an incident. One memorable illustration concerned an upscale candy store where a customer actually spat out a confection onto the floor. The people interviewed were quick to point out that it is rare for shoppers to behave dreadfully. And more than a few noted that bad manners are not restricted merely to foreigners.

Although John can take a photo of a store clerk (he's a much better photographer than me) to illustrate my article and receive as much money with that one click as I do spending the time and effort to interview, write and edit, I don't complain. Our earnings all find their way into the Miller household fund. The editor has asked if I have other article ideas. Wow! I am over the moon and can hardly contain myself.

Stupidity is also a gift of God, but one mustn't misuse it.
                                                    –Pope John Paul II

When in Assisi, Don't Assume Anything

Brimming with new-found confidence over getting one published article under my belt, I immediately start pitching other article ideas. I receive additional assignments from *Wanted in Rome* as well as from other publications including *Transitions Abroad* and a few online magazines. Some assignments don't pan out, though; the Assisi piece is a perfect example.

It all starts very innocently. Santa Dorotea, our little church down the street, was planning a day trip to the town of Assisi, which is best known as the birthplace of St. Francis, the patron saint of Italy. Sounds good to us – a scenic bus ride, nice lunch and back. An easy, simple trip. I decide to pitch the story to an editor, thinking she probably won't be interested. Wrong! She wants me to get "hard news" on the restoration after the earthquake of 1997. She gives me the name of a contact there though she isn't sure he speaks much English. I'm a bit nervous about "hard news" and making an appointment when we're not exactly on our own schedule, so John and I decide to go by ourselves and take the train.

I call the contact to make the appointment, Italian cheat sheet ready to go. The padre is nice and speaks very little English. We agree to meet on the scheduled day at 6:00 p.m. at the "Conference Place." I know I should get more specifics but it is difficult to communicate. I reason that it's a small town and we'll find it with little effort. I take a look at the travel book, which describes Assisi as a lovely town that should be avoided on certain days like the Feast Day of St. Francis, October 4th. Oops. I realize we've already arranged to travel there on that day because it falls on a Friday and John doesn't have classes. We grow worried about packed trains and buses and know there's no way to get a hotel if we are too late and miss our train or bus. Arrangements are set so I call the editor, who is thrilled and wants a first-timer's visit to the Feast Day story.

Fast forward to Friday, the Feast Day. We arrive with no problem, and start asking around for the "Conference Place" – we get directed three different ways. We inquire at the Basilica information booth and are told it is right there and to come back at 6:00 p.m. to meet the padre. We stroll around town, eat a bite, shop and show up at 6:00. But my poor planning or map-reading skill results in completely missing the processional, which is the photo op we need for the Feast Day story. We're trying to figure some other angle when I notice people with news cameras and press passes entering the

"Conference Place," and realize my one-on-one interview is not one-on-one but a real news conference. I wheedle us in and we are given press passes and press kits in Italian about the upcoming International Summit on World Peace!

We are packed into a small room and are listening to the press conference in Italian. I have the deer-caught-in-the-headlights look and my brain is refusing to understand anything so I'm not even taking notes. Then some of the news photographers start panning the room. I figure I'm going to show up on t*ee voo* looking scared out of my wits. I try very hard to look serious and scribble on my press kit sheets. John uses our small digital camera to take some shots.

Finally, the conference concludes and John reminds me to confirm everyone's name and title so we can identify them in the photos. I wouldn't have thought of that, but John has attended hundreds of press conferences during his years working in the news. I don't have any idea what I'm doing and John's wondering how he got put back to work.

I follow a diminutive friar with a kind expression outside who I think speaks English and ask him a question about living like St. Francis in modern times. He says, "Things are different today, we can't live the same life. St. Francis walked everywhere, but the spirit is the same."

John snaps a photo of him and the friar asks me to send him a copy of the article. Later when I review the material in the press kit, I discover the friar is Padre Mizzi, who has just been nominated for the Nobel Peace Prize for the fourth time!

The winner will be announced the following Friday. Later that night, we board the wrong train, which carries our exhausted bodies northward instead of southbound. We finally return home at 2:00 a.m.

When I inform the editor about the press conference on the upcoming International Summit on World Peace and about meeting the Nobel-nominated Padre Mizzi, she seems impressed and says, "You'll have a scoop if he wins and nothing if he doesn't." The next week we find out that Jimmy Carter has won the Nobel Peace Prize.

Ultimately, the article I submitted was never published. It had more to do with me being out of my element and less to do with the awarding of the peace prize. I knew practically nothing about St Francis, *Assisi*, the earthquake that destroyed the precious frescoes and certainly nothing about international press conferences. My piece was a disaster all by itself. I owe my editor a debt of gratitude for rejecting my pitiful submission and saving me from embarrassing myself.

I learned a valuable lesson from this experience. There are good reasons newbies are advised to write what they know — it's easier, more fun and the chances of success are higher.

To him who is determined it remains only to act.

–Italian Proverb

The Bird's the Thing

John and I have been living in Rome for a little over a year and we are growing a bit homesick for some of the American traditions. The first year, we are so caught up in Italian lessons and adjusting to life abroad we barely notice Thanksgiving. It is just another Thursday that we *celebrate* with hamburgers and French fries. But when the second year rolls by, we eagerly agree to turn Thanksgiving into a special day again.

The first step is to buy a turkey and the most logical place to find one is at the supermarket. When I ask the store manager when he would be receiving them, he replies, "*Mai,*" or "Never." Italians don't cook whole turkeys. Ever. It's just not done.

I ask other ex-pats for advice and find a way around this quandary. Whole turkeys can be special ordered in advance from a local butcher. Mauro, the *macellaio* in my neighborhood, is more than happy to oblige. He asks how large a bird I want, and I estimate fifteen pounds or around seven kilos. It will be ready for pick up in one week.

Continuing with Thanksgiving preparations, I find cranberry sauce at a store that specializes in "ethnic" foods, the same place where I regularly purchase peanut butter, a scarce commodity in Rome. I surf the Internet for stuffing recipes and cobble a couple together because I can't find all the ingredients for any one recipe. Green bean casserole proves a little trickier. Instead of the convenience of canned fried onions, I will make my own. Sautéed mushrooms, butter and half-and-half replace canned cream of mushroom soup. Bruna and her husband Alberto, who run the produce booth where I always shop provide the freshest, most perfect green beans I've ever seen.

The day before Thanksgiving I go to pick up the turkey. Mauro smiles proudly as he presents the whole turkey wrapped in butcher paper. I can feel the turkey is soft through the packaging and am surprised that it is fresh, not frozen, and even more surprised that it is much heavier than I expect. I haven't brought the two-wheeled cart I normally use for shopping. Mauro's wife enthusiastically pushes a large bunch of fresh herbs into my hands. "To make the meal more *delizioso*," she says. I thank Mauro, his wife and their grown son, also named Mauro, who all seem just as excited as I am.

By the time I reach my apartment building, my arms feel like they are going to fall off. I struggle to reposition the bag for the three flights of stairs ahead of me when I meet one of my Italian neighbors at the front door, a single mom who has rarely spoken to me. She inquires about the whole turkey and seems impressed that I am going to cook the entire bird. I consider inviting her and her son to join us, but our conversation is brief and she disappears into her apartment before I have a chance.

Thanksgiving morning, I begin preparing the meal. When I unwrap the butcher's packaging from the turkey, I find a fresh, plump turkey. Unlike the turkeys I've purchased in the United States, this turkey lacks a little timer inserted in its side that pops out when it is ready. If the pilgrims managed without a timer, I will too. There is no convenient roasting bag to keep the turkey moist in its own basting bath. I make a few mental adjustments and decide to baste every hour or so while I prepare the side dishes.

When I am finally ready to put the turkey in the oven, I discover it doesn't fit. She (I feel a kinship with her now as we've been through so much) is all dressed up with nowhere to go. After laboring this far, I refuse to be foiled. I look around our apartment for a solution.

When we had first moved in, I re-upholstered the sofa seat cushions. I kept the leftover scraps of material, thinking I might find another opportunity to use them. I pull them out now and begin tearing narrow strips from the bright orange and green material I had purchased at IKEA, autumnal colors no less, and use them to bind the turkey's legs together as tightly as possible. With my turkey bundled and more compact, the oven is the perfect size for me to slip the bird in. She looks a little funny but it works.

That accomplished, I set out to pick up a few ready-made items. From taste-testing experience, I know exactly where to go to get the finishing touches for our feast. My favorite bakery in Piazza San Cosimato supplies olive-topped rolls. From

Checco, a pine-nut torta will substitute nicely for pecan pie. I pick up potatoes and onions at the produce stand just around the corner and return home. As soon as I unlock the heavy wooden door to our building, the delicious aroma of roasting bird seasoned with fresh basil, rosemary, and sage greets me in the stairwell.

We have invited friends: a few American ex-pats and a couple of Italians who have never partaken in a Thanksgiving feast. Iris brings her dog Fidelio along. When they arrive, bearing bottles of Italian wine, we toast our friendship and the blessing of sharing Italy's flavorful bounty.

It doesn't matter when we sit down to dine that our apartment is miniscule or that the strange layout requires schlepping food, beverages and table settings from the kitchen through our bedroom to the dining-living area.

Perhaps the moist, golden-brown turkey tastes so good because of its freshness, the herbs from the butcher's wife, the size of the oven or the way I tightly bound the turkey, or for all these reasons. Whatever the reason, it is without a doubt the best John and I have ever eaten. The green bean casserole, the makeshift stuffing, the special bakery rolls and the pine nut dessert are all delectable—a tribute to the high quality of food and ingredients available in Rome and certainly not my cooking expertise. It is an unforgettable meal, one that we can never replicate. Our Roman holiday will remain etched in our hearts and taste buds forever.

Being a reporter seems a ticket to the world.

–Jackie Kennedy

Drinking Olive Oil in Blue Glasses

When I learned to steer away from subjects I had little knowledge of or interest in, I have better success in getting assignments and having the pieces accepted. I subsequently write about where and how to shop Rome's resale boutiques, Christmas shopping in Trastevere, and how to dress like an Italian – all subjects close to my retail roots.

Another piece about tourists and the souvenirs they buy has me running from the Colosseum to the Vatican and to Trevi Fountain for "research." *Is this really my life!* Sharing a byline with an editor who is planning her wedding in Italy, I contribute with the angle of how to work with an Italian wedding planner. I also write a piece on riding a bike in Rome, a topic inspired by my husband, who navigates Rome and its outskirts on his bicycle several times a week.

It finally dawns on me that presenting myself as a reporter allows me an opportunity to access places and people and experiences I would not normally have, so I start thinking about what I want to do and see and how researching and writing an article can get me there. Iris mentions one day that she has bought some delicious olive oil at a farmers' market in Trastevere and has met the olive orchard owner. I am still impressed by the dizzying number of olive oil choices each time I shop at Standa, and I have always wanted to know why extra virgin olive oil is recommended and of premium quality. Visiting an olive orchard could be fun. I pitch an olive oil story to my editor at *Wanted in Rome*. Amazingly, she tells me they have never covered this topic. Iris calls the orchard owner and asks if I may interview him and then arranges for me to meet him at his home.

Iris, her dog Fidelio, and I take the train to the outskirts of Rome, where Adolfo picks us up. Fidelio and I take the backseat, while Iris sits in the passenger seat so she can translate my questions on the way to Adolfo's home and olive orchard. I take notes along the way, but with the car wending back and forth on the curvy road, I'm getting nauseated.

On the journey to the orchard, we stop to take a photo of the oldest living olive tree in Europe. Fidelio takes this opportunity to poop right in front of the tree! I almost hurl.

With more twisting roads to navigate, we arrive at the family's picturesque stone home in the postcard-perfect hills of Montelibretti. Almost as soon as we step into the dark, cool house we begin drinking olive oil! Not as a beverage, but as a taste test. The proper way to test is to drink the oil from blue glasses that have been warmed by your hands. Blue glass is important to disguise the color of the oil, since I soon discover quality is not determined by color and shouldn't interfere with the rating.

My stomach is still back on the road, but I don't want to offend our hosts, so I drink the warmed oil and nibble the homemade bread offered to cleanse the palate between taste tests. Thinking this is going to cause me to upchuck for sure, it is a pleasant surprise that I don't. I don't even come close. The olive oil is so incredibly good I can't believe it.

Adolfo's olive oil is organic. Organic farmers face the same challenges as conventional farmers, but they choose to do so in a way that they believe is better for the environment, the laborers and, ultimately, the consumer. Adolfo provides specific examples of how organic, or *biologico,* farming differs from conventional methods to produce an extraordinary olive oil.

In the event that pests arrive, a non-toxic treatment is used. Extract of neem, a tropical plant, will repel insects without killing them, as do conventional pesticides. In regard to fertilization, this farm uses *favino*, a broad bean legume. *Favini* are placed on top of the soil to act as a natural fertilizer. Chemical fertilizers force growth, without allowing the necessary time for flavor to develop. So while the end product may look appealing, its taste will often disappoint.

In Italy, a license is required to use chemical pesticides. Dangers for workers include respiratory ailments and heart problems. It's ironic that producing a fruit with so many health benefits could actually be harmful to those who bring it to us. Adolfo observed, "Organic farming is a safeguard for everybody."

Adolfo takes us to the mill, a small stone building, where the olives are transformed into olive oil. When we get out of the car, Adolfo notes that this area is so safe, not only do they not lock their cars but they also leave the keys in the ignition.

I learn much from Adolfo. He tells us progress over the last century in harvesting and processing has greatly improved the quality of the oil that is available today. Olives grow large by August, turning from green to red and then black. Years ago, harvesting was done in January; the theory being that a delayed harvest would glean more oil. Field and laboratory studies later showed that acidity levels actually increased, resulting in an inferior product. Olive farmers now know the optimum time to harvest for oil is between the red and black transition phase, which is usually during October and November.

Any abrasion to the fruit causes oxidation, which begins fermentation, therefore increasing acidity, and is to be avoided whenever possible. The plastic nets commonly seen under trees act as a buffer and as a conduit for collection. In the first half of the last century, processing the harvest usually started ten days after collection. After World War II, pressing began within three to five days. Today, olives are processed within twenty-four hours of harvesting. Once at the mill, the produce is washed gently with water by machine. Another machine slices the olives, even through the pits, and moves the slices to the next phase. Very slowly the pieces are stirred to become a paste. Utmost care is taken to keep them moving and always free from exposure to air.

I am surprised to learn that olives are not pressed. The olive press, which is difficult to clean and bruises the fruit, is now an outmoded piece of equipment. A cylindrical device is now employed instead, which uses centrifugal force to extract the liquid. Once the liquid has been separated it undergoes another session of spinning to separate the oil from the water, which has been added during processing, and the oil is then bottled. All of the modern processing machines are made of steel, because those made of iron leave a metallic taste.

Choosing a bottle from a supermarket shelf can be baffling. Here is a primer:

o   Extra virgin is the best type of olive oil. When a bottle is labeled extra virgin the oil is derived from the first processing of the olives. To be certified, by law it must have a maximum acidity of 1 percent. Some of the more reputable products register well below that level, coming in at below 0.5%.

o   Virgin oil is derived from a subsequent processing of the olives, but still contains only juice from the olives. The acidity level must be between 1 and 2 percent.

o   Plain olive oil uses chemicals to extract the last bit of olive oil from the paste and can therefore not be labeled organic. The oil, which has only 20 to 30 percent olive juice, would be inedible alone, so sometimes a bit of virgin oil is added.

The balance is made up with *olio di olive lampara* or *olio di olive sansa*, which are very low quality oils. This is basically lamp oil.

Before we leave the mill, I ask Adolfo about a truck I saw in the back loaded with remnants of the processed olives and I'm told that's what they use to make the lower quality olive oil. Now I understand why paying more for extra virgin olive oil is absolutely worth it!

Look for a DOP (*Denominazione d'Origine Protetta*) an IGP (*Indicazione Geografica Protetta*) seal attached to the bottle. These testing agencies verify that all the requirements of climate, soil and variety of olives have met their high standards. Products that meet the organic standards will feature the *Agricoltura Biologica* seal.

The trouble with eating Italian food is that five or six days later you're hungry again.

–George Miller

Sunday Lunch with *La Famiglia*

Knowing we will be repatriating in a few months, John and I decide we should export olive oil to the United States. We've got the contact here and have discovered what we believe is a superior product. With Iris's help and my marketing background, it seems like a great idea. Our friend Adolfo agrees to sell to us and we are all invited to the family's home for Sunday *pranzo*, or lunch, to discuss how we will conduct the business.

Iris, John and I arrive by train this time and Adolfo picks us up at the train station and drives us to his home nearby. He points out his girlfriend's house not far from his and she tells me later that it has been in her family forever and is over six hundred years old!

Adolfo's entire family has gathered for Sunday lunch—

father, brothers, their wives, their children, his girlfriend, everyone is here. When lunch is served, I'm so excited to be here that I'm not hungry at all. To not eat is not an option. We throw back a before-dinner drink, then sample antipasti of *polpette* (meatballs), toasts with chicken *pâté,* black and green-olive *pâté* and *suppli* (stuffed rice balls); all paired with white wine.

Then not one, not two, but three types of pasta—spinach ravioli, pasta *dolci* and spaghetti make their way around the table. Entrees include beef, rabbit and chicken fried in what else—olive oil. We later find out Adolfo's mother has used six bottles of olive oil to prepare this meal!

Contorno, or side dishes, consist of fried zucchini, eggplant and mushrooms. We switch to red wine somewhere and then salads signal the end, or so I think.

Doughnuts and fried dough, like piecrust, are first served with an anise-flavored liquor. Then a special brandy is brought out for this occasion.

Espresso is served with the box of chocolates we brought for Adolfo's mother. Several kinds of cheese and fruit are offered, and then after-dinner drinks. I'm so stuffed I don't know how I can eat another bite when Adolfo's aunt plants herself next to me with a dessert tray. Her striking blue eyes twinkle as she watches me try each of the several different types of cookies and candies that she has made herself. I'm afraid of offending her so somehow I sample all of them. They are incredibly good!

As the meal draws to a close, the men are lighting cigars and cigarettes. The smoke swirls around the room, causing me to make a hasty retreat to the bathroom. I don't lose my lunch, but I can't go back to the smoke-encircled table. I use the excuse of taking photos of Adolfo outside to avoid what would surely be seen as the ultimate insult, if not an international incident.

We agree to become business partners and Adolfo says, "We are all friends; let's have a contract so we can all stay friends." Nicely put. Adolfo offers to have the document drawn up and will bring it to Trastevere for us to sign.

Soon after lunch with *la famiglia*, I begin working on getting grocery stores in the United States interested. Adolfo brings me several sample bottles to ship to buyers, and I start pitching large chains in an introductory letter. John and I are thrilled at the thought of becoming independent exporters and creating our own business. We know it won't be easy, but we are undeterred. After already taking a big risk in quitting our jobs and moving to Italy, starting an olive oil import business doesn't seem so scary in comparison. Plus we aren't "investing" a lot of money in it because we don't have a lot of money left.

I have enough money to last me the rest of my life, unless I buy something.

–Jackie Mason

Working: Be It Dollars, Lire or Euros, It All Goes Too Fast

At a Christmas party at the home of one of John's professors, I meet Kate. She is an associate professor that John has met in a class they've taken together. I like her immediately. Kate is a former New Yorker, energetic, animated and full of stories. I get the feeling she comes from a well-to-do family, but prefers to live abroad. In fact, Kate has lived overseas for so long that she speaks English like a second language. Every once in a while she peppers her stories with "*Como si dici...?*" or "How do you say...?" When I get to know her better, I call her on this, saying, "Kate, you're from the United States - you know how to say it." She just laughs in response.

At the party, she tells me she might have a part-time job for me if I am interested. *Am I!* Money has been disappearing faster than we expect during our 21-Month Plan. So much so that "hemorrhaging cash" is a phrase we often use when reviewing our budget.

Kate explains that she has been supplementing her university income by working for an Italian accountant. She says the job consists of teaching her boss English and surfing the Internet looking for American companies wanting to do business in Italy. She says it is easy, and I won't have to speak Italian fluently. Kate has found another part-time job that pays better, but she wants to try it out before quitting her old job. I say, "Call me, please!"

And she does. Kate sets up an interview for me with her boss and she again reassures me my poor command of Italian isn't a problem. For once, I have the perfect outfit to wear—fresh from being altered at the shop down the street, the same one where I landed in slurch. I put together the long black straight skirt, the leather and knitwear cardigan with dozens of tiny silver hooks down the front, add a crisp white blouse, and don my shiny new black leather boots. As I exit our apartment building on the way to the interview, male members of the wait staff of the restaurant directly across the *vicolo,* who are enjoying a break, erupt in applause when they see me in something besides blue jeans and a t-shirt! *Have I achieved the bella figura at last?* I wonder.

At the interview, Kate's boss Giorgio couldn't be nicer. He asks me a few questions, and I feel like it is going well. We talk about me helping him with his English; he adores the language and thinks it is a very beautiful language. I have never thought of English as beautiful, and again see something familiar with a different perspective.

For tutoring, Kate has said all she does is read the *Wall Street Journal* with him and explain any questions he poses. He can already speak English pretty well. We talk about his desire to do business with Americans and how he needs help with marketing his practice. With my marketing background, I am confident I can be of assistance.

For the last question of the interview, Giorgio asks me to speak Italian to him. "Just say anything," he says encouragingly. Caught off guard, I babble a few phrases I have memorized. I'm sure *"Sono andata in palestra,"* my go-to phrase about going to the gym, is in there somewhere. Then I blather on with the most basic, primitive sentences. When I finish my pathetic monologue, I know I'll never get the job. Giorgio has a look of utter disbelief at witnessing the Italian language butchered so brutally. He kindly thanks me for coming in. Interview over.

Kate is standing outside Giorgio's open door so I know she has heard my stammering, the most humiliating moment of the whole ordeal. She tries to keep a straight face as she walks me out of the building, swearing all the time that I haven't done too badly. I know she's lying, and I thank her for thinking of me and offering me the chance to interview, but I am sure I will never hear from Giorgio again.

A few weeks later, I receive a phone call from Giorgio asking me to work for him for a month while Kate is "away in London taking exams of some sort." I can't believe my ears and I am terrified to accept. Part of the job is answering the phones in Italian. Kate has shown me a typed, laminated script they use for this purpose. I could memorize it or just read it and get by.

I try to beg off, but Giorgio insists we give it a try and "see how it goes." I tell him I'll think about it and let him know the next day. I hang up and immediately run downstairs and over to the piazza to Iris's shop to tell her about the offer. She gives me sage advice, "Never turn away from money."

She is right. What do I have to lose? My biggest worry is that I will work the whole month and not get paid. Since I don't have a work permit, I couldn't make a formal complaint if he decides not to pay, but Kate has assured me that he is trustworthy each time I raise this concern.

When I call Giorgio, he is delighted I am taking the job.

So many thoughts run through my mind. *There must be more-qualified candidates than myself. He says I can start working whenever I want. Strange. I say I'll start the first Monday in February. I will get paid by the month, so at least it's the shortest month of the year.*

My first day on the job, Giorgio is leaving the office to pick up his lunch as I arrive and asks if he can bring me back an espresso. I ask for a cappuccino (which is never ordered in the afternoon except by tourists). He laughs and agrees.

Giorgio returns a short time later and hands me the cappuccino, two sugar packets and a napkin. He won't let me reimburse him. He informs me we'll get started after he finishes eating lunch in his office. This is to become our routine the entire time I work for Giorgio—a cappuccino brought to me piping hot every day when I arrive for work. *Ahhhhh, Italians know how to run a business.*

Part of my job is to review the day's mail with Giorgio, read any letters in English and determine whether he needs to respond to them. We read a tiny portion of the *Wall Street Journal*, taking turns reading the front-page blurbs and then later, I pick out the most interesting stories to me and suggest we read those articles. It is eye opening for both of us. There are more ways of saying business is up or down than I have ever realized: growing, slipping, struggling, dropping, expanding, bolstering, atrophying, rising, trailing, increasing, falling, recovering, gaining, lowering, pushing higher, reducing, faltering, declining, deflating, stemming, collapsing and eroding. And then there are even more descriptive ones, including flowering, clawing back, on the rocks, tumbling and facing a headwind.

Cultural differences show up now and then when reading from an Italian's perspective. For example, *chiocciola* is the Italian word for snail. It is also what Italians call the "@" sign. So when an article mentions sending snail mail, Giorgio assumes that means sending an email - a charming, if not, understandable assumption.

6 February 2003

Giorgio and I quickly fall into a routine. After our English tutoring session ends, I start surfing the Internet and get used to my new office surroundings. Kate's desk is one of two in the foyer of Giorgio's office. Francesca, a bookkeeper, has the other desk, but she only works mornings. Kate's desk is next to the window so I have a scenic view of other buildings and plenty of afternoon sunlight. I enjoy having a desk with a computer and a large monitor that is mine for a few hours each day. John and I share a laptop at home, and we only have the living room table for workspace, which must be cleared off for every meal.

Giorgio's office is located in Prati, the same upscale neighborhood where I took Italian lessons with Daniele. It's an easy bus ride to get here. The office is in an old palazzo where you must be buzzed in. Then you take the elevator or walk up the gleaming, polished marble staircase. Other business and medical offices are housed here as well, and they all share a central courtyard with trees and a green space.

Nicolette is from France and the morning girl hired to do the same thing as me except, instead of teaching English, she teaches Giorgio French. We're always passing each other in the entryway as Nicolette's shift ends and mine begins, and her command of English is about as good as my Italian so we don't get to dish near enough.

Nicolette is an attractive blonde. One day as we're switching shifts, she tells me a story about how Giorgio propositioned her. At least that's what I think she is saying. To make sure, I ask her if he said, "*Voulez-vous coucher avec moi?*"

It is perhaps the best French phrase I know thanks to Labelle, and at least it is the question I want to ask.

"No, no," she laughs.

Nicolette explains she was engaged at the time Giorgio asked her to have a drink with him, bourbon to be exact. Nicolette made it clear that she would not be going for drinks with him, and she made it clear to me that her then-fiancé was not happy with this arrangement at all.

Giorgio is not without female companionship though. Kate has informed me he is having an affair with a married woman. He is even having the other end of the office renovated into a little *appartamento,* because where else would a nearly forty-year-old, single Italian man who still lives with his parents bring his married lover?

By the end of February, Giorgio hasn't heard a peep from Kate and neither have I. E-mails I send to her for Giorgio go unanswered. She also doesn't reply to my personal emails and phone calls. It doesn't look as if Kate will be returning, so Giorgio asks me to continue working for him. Since almost no one ever comes into the office, the phone hardly rings, and no one from the States emails back, I hold onto this job for two more months. I think Giorgio really just likes having company because I never see him do any real work—it must be that Francesca is responsible for keeping the office running.

None of us knows what has happened to Kate, or why she left us all hanging, but weeks later Francesca spots Kate on a busy city bus. Francesca doesn't have the opportunity to talk to her, so the mystery remains unsolved, especially since Kate previously supplied the story that she is in London finishing her studies.

In April, Giorgio asks me to help him find a replacement since I'll soon be moving back to the U.S. after John graduates in May. I place an ad and we are inundated with résumés. Finding a job in Italy is difficult anyway, and to find one that doesn't require a work permit and that requests a native English speaker is all the more rare.

I am shocked at some of the high-caliber résumés we receive. Résumés that make me wonder why these people are applying for such a lowly position. They hold advanced degrees, are fluent in Italian and many times a few other languages. One particular outstanding applicant has written an addendum to the Italian dictionary, for Pete's sake! Not all are stellar though. Another applicant whose native language is not English sends her résumé, a typo-ridden cover letter, and a cheerleader-type photo of herself.

Giorgio asks me to set up interviews for several candidates, including the dictionary- addendum writer and the cheerleader. When I protest the cheerleader by holding up her cover letter with eleven red-circled mistakes, Giorgio shrugs and says, "I think we should give her a chance."

One aside about hiring in Italy: There is no such thing as politically correct. Classified ads often include preferences for personal attributes, such as height requirement, hair color, even age.

I meet with the candidates for preliminary interviews and then Giorgio conducts his own interviews. The addendum writer is impressive. She is my top pick though I hate to see her talent and skills wasted on a job that will never go anywhere. The cheerleader is cute and likeable and not that fluent in English. I can't believe it when Giorgio asks me to set up a second appointment with her. I think he is going to offer her the job, but she never returns and never calls to cancel. We never hear from her again.

During the interviewing process, one candidate arrives while Giorgio is out running an errand. Giorgio asks me to proceed with the interview and he will plan to be back to complete the second round. This young woman and I talk and talk and talk, but Giorgio does not return. He is probably the only young Italian who doesn't own a cell phone. I continually apologize for his tardiness, saying, "He is never late like this. I can't imagine why he's not back."

Finally, Giorgio returns and he is soaking wet. Someone has stolen his *motorino* and he has had to walk back from his errand in the rain. Not missing a beat, with his clothes and hair dripping all over the furniture and the tile floor, he dives into introductions and interviews the candidate,

After work, Giorgio goes back to where his *motorino* was stolen and looks all around. He visits the same spot a few days later and, believe it or not, finds it returned *sans petrol*. After running out all the gas, the culprit has left the *motorino* right back at the crime scene.

In the meantime, the addendum writer has diligently followed up with us regarding the status of the open position. She has aced the interview, is by far the most qualified candidate, and is eventually offered the job.

Cock your hat—angles are attitude.

–Frank Sinatra

A Custom-Made Italian Suit

The idea of the *bella figura* doesn't apply only to women. Looking great is just as important for Italian men—and men who have lived here for almost twenty-one months. In April, with just a few weeks left in Italy, I decide to splurge on a special graduation present for John—a handmade Italian suit. Giorgio owns several and I often compliment him on them. He recommends his tailor to us and even calls and makes an appointment for the initial fitting.

Giorgio says they will charge €780 for a suit coat and pants. With the favorable exchange rate nearing parity, that converts to roughly $780 in U.S. dollars. While that is still a sizable chunk, the value of a custom-made Italian suit will pay for itself many times over. Plus we have the advantage of being in Italy for several more weeks for the additional fittings required. I rationalize that if I hadn't gotten the job with Giorgio, we wouldn't have this money to spend anyway, and we will never have an opportunity like this again. Besides, John's tall, thin cycling physique is not easy to fit off the rack and alterations can only do so much. No, this will be a very special gift, a suit that he can use for interviews and for special occasions for years to come. We are told it will take about a month and involve three fittings to complete the suit.

The first visit begins awkwardly. We are nervous and it takes a little doing for us to even find the tailor's shop, which is on the other side of the Tiber from Prati, tucked in a little neighborhood. Once there, we have to explain who we are, which shouldn't have been too hard, but they don't seem to be expecting us. Maybe it's us showing up at the appointed time, which is very un-Italian, that throws them off. Whatever the reason, it seems we aren't making a great first impression.

We are invited to step into the shop but there is nowhere to go and nowhere to sit. My shoulders automatically hunch, as I am taller than both of the tailors. We feel like clunky interlopers standing in the middle of their tiny shop amid bust forms with half-made suits and stacks of fabrics. No one seems to know what to say or how to start. Luigi, who appears to be the head tailor, makes an effort to smile every so often, which makes us feel a bit less intrusive.

I think we will be able to point to pictures and fabric and that they would measure and we'd do okay, but it is more difficult than I had imagined.

John is more confident with his Italian skills than I am because he has continued to advance with his college courses. He also does very well getting by and conversing in Roman bicycle shops. I have pretty much given up on formal classes by now and am getting by with what I call "shopping Italian." I know what to say to buy pretty much anything anywhere. Also,

I have honed my skills as I write articles on particular topics and have learned the lingo needed to conduct interviews. Discussing the details of a tailor-made suit for John in this little shop is unlike anything similar to pointing to salmon or gnocchi and asking *"per due persone."* We don't command the Italian vocabulary we need here.

The tailors confer with each other and begin to try to converse with us. Their dialect differs from what we hear in Trastevere even though our neighborhood lies only about three miles south from here. John and I grasp for common words to try to interpret their comments or questions. We are utterly lost.

The tailors, probably in their seventh decade, speak not one word of English, not that we expect them to. They don't seem in any hurry and the awkward moments drag on while we stammer for common understanding. According to Giorgio, they are winding down, retired for the most part. They still make custom suits for special clients like Giorgio, and I guess now, Giorgio's friends.

I try calling Giorgio at his office to come help us, but he doesn't answer. He still doesn't carry a cell phone so we are helpless. Luigi leads us to stacks of bolts of gray, navy, brown and black materials and flips up the edges so we can run our hands across the fabric and feel the weight of the pin stripes, windowpanes, glen plaids and solids. I assume Luigi is asking us to pick a fabric. We are undecided as to which weight to choose since we will be moving to Syracuse, New York, for the next year (more on this later), but then probably end up back in Texas for the long term. We are about to commit to a style and a fabric and spend hundreds of euros and we have no idea what we are going to end up with. I am imagining a €780 mistake when the buzz of Giorgio's *motorino* roars through the open window. *Grazie a Dio!* Giorgio has come to our rescue!

Welcomed warmly by the tailors and us, Giorgio quickly smoothes over our rough start, even helping us choose something he describes as "elegante." Giorgio suggests a mid-weight, solid, charcoal gray, wool gabardine. The jacket will be single breasted with three buttons and side vents and finished off with a subtle striped lining. The trousers will have tapered legs and cuffs. Luigi measures John and we are done—for now. John will have to come back for two more fittings over the next few weeks.

I know it is going to be a gorgeous suit—Giorgio has great taste and I can't have more confidence in these two experienced artisans. I can't wait to see John in this suit at graduation.

The toilets at a local police station have been stolen. Police say they have nothing to go on.

–Ronnie Barker, British Comedian

Nothing Brings Neighbors Together Like Shared Sewer Lines

With just a few precious days left in Rome, the landlord decides to rip out our toilet and redo the plumbing. When the workers arrive, they have to completely remove the toilet and tiles and redo everything. We are told that this job will take at least two days.

When I think back, Signora Oberti seemed to have asked about our plumbing a time or two, but I never fully grasped the extent of her concern. Apparently there has been a problem for some time and it has impacted more than just Signora Oberti. Finally, after twenty-one months, every neighbor in the building makes the trek to our door and through our apartment to see the work in progress—a hole in our floor so large we can wave to Signora Oberti down below. It isn't until one neighbor—the meticulously groomed woman in her sixties

I've nicknamed Ms. Sophisticate who would never acknowledge us—traipses through our living room and bedroom to the bathroom that we discover she speaks impeccable English.

Our next-door neighbors who speak not a word of English, but have greeted us with warm smiles for twenty-one months, invite us to use their facilities anytime day or night. Using gestures, they let us know their door will remain unlocked for us. They give us a tour of their home, so we will know, literally, where to go.

When we move back to the U.S we will need a car. John has decided to go to graduate school and has been accepted at S.I. Newhouse School of Public Communications in Syracuse, New York. He has been offered a teaching-assistant position, which will defray some of the costs and is a great opportunity. We'll need to buy a vehicle and that is the very last thing I want to spend money on. John talks to his dad one night and learns he will be selling his twenty-year-old Toyota truck. We decide we should ask to buy it if John's dad hasn't already sold it. When we find out it is available and we have enough money to buy it I am elated. When I tell Sherry of my relief in buying a twenty-year-old truck, she replies emphatically, "This experience has grounded you!"

And she is right. From a girl who wouldn't ride a city bus four miles to work in Houston, to one that has navigated subways, trams and buses, and has happily worn the soles out of several pairs of shoes, walking hundreds of miles over the past twenty months, I will never feel the same way about transportation.

My last car, a Nissan Altima purchased brand new, was the nicest car I'd ever owned—but now, I could not care less about automatic windows and power steering.

Everything is happening fast now. Besides our apartment being a repair mess, we have a long list of To-Do's before our repatriation—hmmm, just like before we started this adventure. We have to return the modem, disconnect Internet service, get the final fitting for John's suit, pack and ship a box of stuff that won't fit in our suitcases, book flights to Syracuse to look for a place to live, meet with Iris and Adolfo to sign the olive-oil export business contract, ship sample olive oil bottles to the U.S., not to mention the primary reason we've been here for twenty-one months, attend John's graduation.

Plus it's time again for the Roma Komen Race for the Cure and we've organized our own group this year. John's sister and her husband are coming for graduation and I've signed them up along with John and myself. Natalie, our friend who was here the first year and who went through 9/11 with us, has moved to London. She's coming back to visit and to run the race too, as is Kim, the young woman who replaced Natalie at the university.

I had hoped to have a chunk of cash left to make our transition back to the U.S. easier. We don't, so I am squeezing every centesimo out of the euros we have.

While we've been careful not to buy too much since we have little room to store anything, we do pick up a few mementos: colorful pottery from the trip to Taormina, books (mostly Italian cookbooks and books about Italy since I utilized the Santa Susanna Library as much as possible), a few clothes, the black leather boots, and winter coats for each of us. Mine is a chic, black, pea-coat that I just had to have, and John's is a gorgeous, charcoal grey wool coat—a splurge the first winter.

We are going to have to ship all this before we leave so I contact an international moving company located near Fiumicino Airport. We have to change our plane tickets because the airline has us routed through Detroit, which John thinks is ridiculous. Since we're already at the airport making these arrangements, we call the moving company and the owner offers to pick us up and bring us to his office to discuss the cost to ship our belongings. It's always easier to negotiate in person, and I drive a hard bargain to get the best possible price. Also, John has purchased another bike while we've been here, so we are having it packed and shipped too.

The moving company sends a shipping box to the apartment a few days later. I carefully choose what goes and what stays. Denim-looking, soft *"matriamoniale"* bed sheets, sheets sized for a full bed, and a fluffy throw, unfortunately, don't make the cut. I leave one of our Italian dictionaries on purpose, almost as a tradition. The apartment had a few when we arrived from previous study-abroad students so it seemed like the thing to do – a sort of changing of the guard if you will.

A Sicilian once told me, "Italians don't move a lot." During our first year in Rome, I was planning the pre-Christmas trip to Taormina and was making hotel reservations by phone. The reservationist spoke English very well, and she had time to talk. She asked me why I was living in Rome and where I was from. She listened to my story and then said, "Italians are not like that. You're born in a place. You live in that place, and you die in that place." What wonderful simplicity. I have never considered staying in one place forever.

I am used to moving. I have done so more than a dozen times since graduating from college. I always look forward to my next new apartment, new neighborhood, new city and new job. This time feels different, however, and not just because it is an international move. No big surprise here—I really love living in Italy. I am very much looking forward to seeing my family and friends and visiting our favorite restaurants in Montrose, our old neighborhood in Houston, but I'm not ready to move back to the U.S. Maybe if we were moving to Houston, it would have felt like going home, but we are going to be living in Syracuse, New York, for the next fourteen months while John completes grad school, with no clear destination beyond that timeframe.

But what nags at me the most is my impending loss of independence. In Rome, I have independence because the city offers a level of convenience and freedom I've never experienced anywhere else. I feel safe in my neighborhood, being able to go anywhere I want at any time. Need a gelato fix at 11:00 p.m.? No problem. If John is studying and doesn't want to come along, I can just run down the stairs and stroll around the neighborhood and over to Viale Trastevere to one of our favorite artisanal gelato shops. I can enjoy the walk home, and often run into someone I know. I never worry about my personal safety. I know I will miss this when I return to the U.S. I also have no idea what to expect of life in the U.S. after 9/11. Everyone says life there will never be the same.

* * *

Flight plans change again. Our Tuesday flight scheduled for May 20, the last day we can be in our apartment, is cancelled, so the airline rebooks us on a flight one day earlier. I do not want to complain about having one less day in Italy after having twenty-one months, but we are hustling to get everything done on time and this ratchets everything up a few notches. Not to mention the university has asked us to move to a hotel on Monte Gianicolo for two nights while the workers retile and finish fixing the plumbing problem in our bathroom.

We go for the last fitting, or what we believe is the final try-on for John's suit, but the suit is not finished. We are just a couple of days away from the graduation ceremony and are told the suit will not be ready for another week. We panic and try to explain that we need it by Friday, but Luigi just shakes his head and holds his hands up as if there is nothing he can do.

Giorgio calls Luigi and implores him to finish the suit in time for John's graduation in two days. The rapid-fire conversation goes on and on and I'm holding my breath that Giorgio will be able to persuade him to finish in time. Even if they can't have the suit ready for graduation, a week is still too late. We're departing Rome on Monday, only four days away.

Luigi finally agrees but will charge extra for the "rush." We can live with that. He only asked for another €20. I pick the suit up on graduation day, amid a bunch of other errands and race back to the apartment. John slips the suit on and it not only fits him perfectly, but it also looks "elegant." On further examination of the suit, we see that every seam is beautifully hand finished. The tailors have hand stitched their own label into the suit coat. Giorgio's choice in the fabric, the design and the tailors' work is beyond impeccable. This bespoke suit is worth every *centesimo* - and the last-minute drama!

On the other hand, I haven't given one thought about what I will wear to John's graduation until it is too late. I have absent-mindedly packed away my nicer dresses in the box already given to the international shipper. I cobble together an outfit from the mix-and- match pieces I've kept behind and don't feel *bella figura* at all, but at this point what can I do? I am so proud of John; he has worked hard to earn this degree, and we both have made many sacrifices to get here! I put on my make-do outfit, pay extra attention to my makeup, put my hair up in a twist and smile. Nothing can spoil this day.

A few hours before we need to leave for graduation, I stop by Roberto and Anna's small specialty grocery outside of Standa where I regularly pick up pesto Genovese, the most delectable olives, and cheeses that they would recommend and that I might never have heard of otherwise. We hug good-bye – they always have such beautiful smiles—and that's all I can manage. I walk one last time through the streets of our neighborhood and through Piazza Santa Maria in Trastevere and I can hardly believe twenty-one months have flown by so quickly. I love this place with all its beauty and its imperfections. The glistening mosaics, the octagonal fountain, the scaffolding still in place on the nearby building, the gelato shops, the *giornalaio* and the *arrotino,* and the *punkabbestia* and their dogs. I'm going to miss it all.

What will this neighborhood look like when we come back in five years? Ten years? We don't know when we'll be back — if ever. But I try not to think about that. I can't. The major sites will surely still be here. It will still take the same number of steps to walk from Trastevere to the Vatican. Some things will change; of course, nothing can stay exactly the same. Will Maria and Aldo still be living upstairs? Signora Oberti's grandsons will be taller if not all grown up. And dozens of visiting students and professors will have lived in our *appartamento*. I hope they enjoy it as much as we have.

18 May 2003

The night before we depart Rome, we attend a going-away dinner with many of our friends at Conte di Monte Christo, the restaurant right across from our apartment. Iris, Marty and Sherry, Natalie, a university friend Rosalba and her fiancé, even John's sister and her husband from Austin are here. The night air is just right so all the doors and windows to the restaurant have been flung open. Dinner *al fresco* with friends and family is the perfect way to spend the last evening of our twenty-one-month Roman life.

We have shared just a moment in Rome's nearly three-thousand-year history, but she will resonate in us for the rest of our lives.

Travel is more than the seeing of sights, it is a change that goes on, deep and permanent, in the ideas of living.

–Miriam Beard

Arrivederci, a Presto!

19 May 2003

At 4:00 a.m. on the day of our departure, as we begin taking our suitcases downstairs to meet the cab that will take us to the airport, Signora Oberti's door swings open. She and Federico have risen to send us off with espresso and pastries. She hugs me over and over, and I have much I want to say, but the cab driver begins honking and yelling, the sounds echoing through the stairwell. It is reminiscent of our first encounter with Signora Oberti, only then it was Birillo, Signora Oberti's dog doing the bellowing.

After all these months, it's the bum's rush out of town. John and I gulp the hot beverages and practically swallow whole the soft, breakfast cakes. More hugs and tears and promises to return, and we are gone. Poof. We don't live here anymore.

Our ride to Fiumicino takes bad Roman driving to a whole new level. We learn the cab driver has another customer to pick up after us and he's already running late. Our stop at Signora Oberti's puts him even further behind and he's really gunning it. John and I want to savor this moment, but instead we fear for our lives. There's no time for sentimentality as I imagine the car crashing a dozen different ways. After living life at a slower pace, this is hardly the romantic way I expect our last few minutes in Rome to unfold. Life is not always what we plan or expect and that is where the adventure comes in. A sleepy, calm ride to the airport would most certainly have been forgotten, or worse, it might have turned into too much of a weepy, sentimental moment. I probably needed that jolt of adrenaline to keep from losing all composure.

Our flight to New York has one stop, Amsterdam. We have a couple of hours on the ground here, and I'm stubbornly lugging a pair of heavy bags with a few gifts and a couple of new outfits so I can get the VAT (Value Added Tax) refund. I have to present the merchandise and receipts before we leave the European Union to qualify for the refund.

When I come round the corner to the Global Refund Desk, I can't believe my eyes. It's Massimo; rather, the actor that portrays Massimo on *The Bold & the Beautiful*. How perfect! Without thinking, I call him by his character's name and he turns and smiles. The actor's name is Joe Mascolo and when he finishes his transaction, I ask him if we can take his picture. He is extremely nice and poses with me, and then he spends several minutes talking with John and me asking where we are going and where we came from. I tell Mr. Mascolo about watching *Beautiful* in Rome dubbed in Italian, and how it gave me and my favorite neighbor such pleasure to discuss the plot lines. Imagining sending these photos with my first letter to Signora Oberti comforts me the rest of the way home.

Epilogue

After life in Rome, we spent a little over a year in Syracuse, New York, where John received a Master's degree from S. I. Newhouse School of Media Management. The olive oil exporting enterprise was short lived as shipping costs and insurance thwarted any hope of making a profit.

Eventually settling back in Texas, we welcomed our son Nate in 2005. We live in San Antonio, where John coincidentally works for a sister school of his Italian university. I continue to write freelance and also work for an online service that provides rewards for taking public transportation, carpooling, biking and walking.

3

ACKNOWLEDGMENTS

In soloing—as in other activities—it is far easier to start something than it is to finish it.

—Amelia Earhart

Finishing this book was much more difficult than giving up a steady paycheck, leaving everything familiar and moving to a foreign country. I would never have continued without the encouragement of my husband John Miller who believed I could do it and kept telling me, "Write it for Nate, at least this will explain where his inheritance went."

To my son Nate Miller, your hugs and enthusiasm kept me going on many days. I love you to pieces. I hope this book inspires you to follow your dreams no matter how impossible they may seem.

To my mother, Billie Supeter and my sister Marilyn Gilchrist, I can't wait to share this book with you! Mom, thank you for suggesting we take the bus that day in Florence; it was a game changer. Marilyn, thank you for being a wonderful sister and for not asking when the book would be done. :-)

My life is enriched on a daily basis by friends I feel blessed to have. Cynthia Shepherd and Suzy Maloch, thank you for your perpetual enthusiasm for this project, and for offering to store the stuff we couldn't bear to part with. Sherry Bushue, Terri Schexnayder and Elaine Davenport – thank you for treating me like a "real writer" when I hadn't gotten there myself yet. Robyn Nosari, Kaci Goodman and Shana Prichard – thank you for offering to read the first chapters and asking for more. Molly Zaldivar, *grazie mille* for reading the manuscript with an Italian perspective and making priceless edits.

Without my brilliant writing partner Joanne Liu, this book would have been nothing more than a compilation of articles and not a story. Thank you for helping me realize what it could be, for smoothing out all the rough parts, and for making me laugh all along the way. Rebecca Ponton, your enthusiasm made all the difference in getting this book to the finish line. Thanks for the bean and cheese tacos! Marty Bushue, thank you for the use of your charming photo of our building's doorway for the cover.

Special thanks to Shawn Mihalik and Bradford Gantt for going above and beyond in creating a beautiful interior and gorgeous cover for this book. Your patience astounds.

And lastly, a warm thank you to all the readers of my Italy articles who shared with me their own dreams to live abroad. Your interest in our adventure inspired me to share the details of our life in another country, culture and language. I hope this book gives you and all my new readers the courage to live your dreams. Let me know how it goes: Martha at timesnewromanbook.com

ABOUT THE AUTHOR

Martha Miller is a former retail marketing executive turned freelance writer and essayist. Her work has appeared in *Transitions Abroad, Wanted in Rome, LifeinItaly.com, GoNomad.com, Go World Travel, International Living, Family Circle, Parents, The Christian Science Monitor* and *The Writer*. Her personal essays and syndicated columns, *Living Greenly* and *Living Online*, have been published in regional publications across the United States.

To see pictures of the Millers' apartment in Rome and other favorite photos from their Italy adventure visit

http://timesnewromanbook.com

CPSIA information can be obtained
at www.ICGtesting.com
Printed in the USA
FFOW02n0059090817
38646FF